# CHALDEAN NATION:
# Past and Present

**By Fr. Michael J. Bazzi**

San Diego, California
2022

**Chaldean Nation**
© 2022 by Michael J. Bazzi
Edited by Sally Ades
Cover by Amy Grigoriou
ISBN: 978-1-941464-44-1
PCCN: Library of Congress Control Number: Pending

All Rights Reserved. Printed in the United States of America. No part of this book may be used or reproduced in any manner whatsoever without written permission except in the case of brief quotations embodied in critical articles and reviews.

## PUBLISHED BY

Let in the Light Publishing

www.letinthelightpublishing.com

# Photo and Illustration Credits

Cover: Babylon Gate, © Karrar A. Alawadi

Page 28: "Christ Crucified" by Antonello da Messian, 1475. Permission © The National Galley, London.

Page 46: Assyrian Winged Bulls Gurading Nineveh © Babin.

Page 46: Map of the Last Mesopotamian Empire; p.52 Good Morning Babylonia Chaldean Alphbet Chart; p.53 Map of Mesopotamian pre-Historic Sites; p.55 Map of Ancient Mesopotamian Cities; p.54 Map of Ancient Mesopotamian; Permission © Amer Hanna Fatuhi.

All other images are used with permission © Bernadit Seman.

# Contents

Foreword ............................................................................... 7

Introduction ........................................................................... 9

Chapter 1 - The Chaldeans' Country ................................... 11

Chapter 2 - Chaldean Empire – Neo Babylonians .............. 15

Chapter 3 - The Chaldean Church ....................................... 24

Chapter 4 - The Chaldean Church in the World .................. 27

Chapter 5 - The Chaldean Church in the United States ..... 29

Chapter 6 – The Chaldean Catholic Community in San Diego ....... 32

Chapter 7- The Eastern Catholic Churches ........................ 43

Chapter 8 - The Chaldean Rite ............................................ 46

Chapter 9 - Aramaic – Language of the Chaldeans ........... 48

Appendix - A ........................................................................ 52

Appendix - B ........................................................................ 54

Bibliography ......................................................................... 56

About the Author ................................................................. 57

# Foreword

Rev. Fr, Michael Bazzi is a genuine son of the Chaldean Nation and an authentic priest of the Catholic Church.

This book is a compendium of the actual dispersion of the Chaldean people written by a loyal and competent son who has served his nation and church faithfully for more than 57 years in Tilkepe (Iraq), Detroit (Michigan), and San Diego (California).

Bishop Sarhad Y. Jammo, San Diego, California, 2021.

# Introduction

In the Old and New Testaments of the Bible, the name of the Chaldeans is of great importance. The name of the Chaldeans is mentioned 70 times, the name of the Chaldean Emperor Nebuchadnezzar 111 times, the name Kaldu 14 times, Kaldani 13 times, Ur of the Chaldeans 4 times, Babylon 300 times, and Babylonians 21 times.

Here are some excerpts from the sayings of the prophets. Among them are the great prophets: 1) Isaiah prophesied from 740-681 B.C. in Jerusalem; 2) Jeremiah prophesied from 627-587 B.C. in Jerusalem; 3) Ezekiel prophesied from 593-571 B.C. in Babylon; and 4) Daniel who prophesied from 605-535 B.C. in Babylon.

These prophets mentioned in their prophecies the Chaldeans and their emperor, Nebuchadnezzar. Isaiah and Jeremiah wrote and prophesied in Jerusalem, while Ezekiel and Daniel accompanied the exiles in their youth to Babylon, lived and prophesied and died in Babylon, the capital city of the Chaldeans.

**Isaiah:** 19:13: Isaiah calls Babylon the adornment of the kingdoms and the splendor of the Chaldeans' pride.

**Jeremiah 25:8:** "Says the Lord: Behold, I will send Nebuchadnezzar king of Babylon my servant, and bring him into this land, which I will make a desolate land, and it shall be enslaved to the king of Babylon seventy years."

**Jeremiah 37:8:** "Thus says the Lord, 'The Chaldeans who fought against Egypt and were victorious will come to Jerusalem and burn it.'"

**Jeremiah 6:38:** The chiefs of the Jews threw Jeremiah into the dungeon in Jerusalem, and when Nebuchadnezzar arrived, he took him out of the well and freed him.

**Jeremiah 51:7:** The best summary of the Chaldean rule came in his description of Babylon to the Chaldeans as "a golden cup in the hand of the Lord that makes all the earth drunk."

**Ezekiel 11:17:** wrote, "The word of the Lord came to me, saying: 'Say to the house of rebellion: Behold, the king of Babylon has come to Jerusalem, and has taken its king and the great men of the earth.'"

**Ezekiel 3:21:** "The Lord said the sword of the king of Babylon will be upon Judah and Jerusalem" See also 2 Kings chapter 25.

**Ezekiel 29:19:** "Thus says the Lord: Behold, I give to Nebuchadnezzar king of Babylon the land of Egypt."

**Ezekiel 30:24:** "The Lord said, I will strengthen the arm of the king of Babylon, and put my sword in his hand, and break the arms of Pharaoh" and the prophet calls the Chaldeans, "giants."

**Ezekiel 32:11:** "The Lord said: 'The sword of the king of Babylon will come upon you, and I will bring down your multitude with mighty swords."

Daniel the Prophet lived at the court of Nebuchadnezzar in Babylon as an advisor. In chapters 1-4 of Daniel, most of his writings are about Nebuchadnezzar. The most beautiful of what he wrote: "Nebuchadnezzar, after witnessing how God saved the three young men from the hellfire, prayed saying: 'I, Nebuchadnezzar, praise and glorify the King of Heaven, whose works are all true and His ways are just.'"

Interestingly, the Bible makes King Nebuchadnezzar one of God's favorite servants, as God helped him even though he was not from the chosen people, to take the chosen people and use them to achieve God's purposes.

Concerning the description of the Chaldean soldiers, the prophet Habakkuk, a minor prophet who died in 589 B.C., wrote, 1: 6-10: Thus says the Lord: I will raise up the Chaldeans, the people who walk in the breadth of the earth faster than tigers, their horses and faster than wolves. In the evening their horses leap, and their knights come from afar. They fly like an eagle in a hurry to swallow. They each come from the east, and the beginning of their common appearance is a gale wind that piles upon the captives like sand. They mock kings and princes, they are a laughingstock. They laugh at any fortress. They pass like the wind and pass.

# Chapter I
# The Chaldeans' Country

The diaspora Christian Catholic Chaldean community emigrated originally from the great country of Mesopotamia: the land between the Tigris and the Euphrates Rivers or modern "Iraq." It is part of the Fertile Crescent, which is called, "the Cradle of Civilization." This gave birth to the political, judicial, religious, and military systems that steered earlier societies on a course that would eventually lead to our modern world's intricate system of nations, states, and countries.

The Book of Genesis places the Garden of Eden in Mesopotamia. The great Hanging Gardens of Babylon built by the Chaldean Emperor Nebuchadnezzar II around 600 B.C. for his wife, Amitas, were also chosen as one of the Seven Ancient Wonders of the World.

**Prehistoric events:** Our present knowledge of ancient Mesopotamia, the cradle of civilization, rests almost exclusively on the study of the written documents and artifacts recovered by archaeologists from the ruined city mounds of Mesopotamia during the last 150 years.

Throughout antiquity, the civilization of the inhabitants of Mesopotamia played the leading role in Near Eastern politics, art, science, philosophy, religion and literature.

Not much is known about the first settlers of Mesopotamia. There are traces of hunter-gatherers and cattle breeders from as early as 10,000 B.C. These were followed by farmers of grain and other plants. Remains of inhabited villages have been discovered which date from 6,000 B.C. According to historians, the two oldest villages of Mesopotamia were Hassuna near Nineveh in the north of Mesopotamia and Tall Sawar near Samarra, in the middle of Mesopotamia.

The following are the main prehistoric culture stages:

| | | |
|---|---|---|
| In the North: | JARMO | 7,000 B.C. |
| | HASSUNA | 6,000 B.C. |
| | SAMARRA | 5,500 B.C. |
| | HALAL and ERIDU | 5,000 B.C. |

In the South:   UBAID                4,500 B.C.
                URUK                 3,500 B.C.


## Recorded events from the Fourth to the Third Millennium B.C.:

This era marked the end of the prehistoric period. The historical era began with the first appearance of useable writing. The Sumerians were credited with the creation of this first system of writing around 3,200 B.C.

Mesopotamia is where the first form of writing was created and used. It is the place where the wheel was first invented and where the first known law code was established by the famous king of Babylon, Hammurabi. Ancient Mesopotamia gave the world the basic principles of mathematics: the 60-minute hour, the 360-degree circle, astronomy and astrology. Lastly, it is where Aramaic, the language of Christ Jesus and the New Testament flourished and became the lingua franca of the Middle East in the seventh century B.C.

Archaeology reveals that around 3500 B.C. the world's first cluster of cities arose in ancient Mesopotamia. They were cities with names such as Ur (of the Chaldeans), Eridu and Uruk (from which the name Iraq may have been derived). City-states joined into kingdoms under the most powerful rulers, whose territorial aggression expanded their domain into the first empire: the great empire of Sargon of Akkad, whose armies pushed into Lebanon, Anatolia (Turkey), and Persia around 2300 B.C.

Technology has also played its role in Mesopotamia. The long range of the composite bow enabled King Sargon to usher in the first missile age. Metallurgy (the science of metals) started when the first plowshare was invented. The plowshare helped fill the fields with grain and also aided in forging weapons. Many things came into creation after the foundation of metallurgy: they used a potter's wheel to make a chariot, and iron and bronze to make swords and spears for fighting. Writing first appeared in Mesopotamia about 3500 B.C. In the early days, Mesopotamian writing took the form of abstract symbols known as cuneiform (also known as wedge writing). This opened the door to written history and other scholarship, including the map of the world.

Astrology began in the third millennium B.C. in Ur of the Chaldeans though the earliest evidence of it is on clay tablets in Babylon. The Mesopotamian ziggurats, such as the Tower of Babel, were built with clay brick tablets. Platforms were built to observe the stars and cast horoscopes.

Ancient Mesopotamian cosmology is still the basis of present-day astronomy. Shamash, the sun god and lawgiver, ruled the day while the moon god, Sin, ruled the night. They moved along the heavenly equator named after another god, Anu. Hence, the influence of the sun and moon along the ecliptic goes back to Babylon. At first, however, astrology only foretold the fate of the monarch and the state, not individuals. During the Hellenistic period (fourth to the first centuries B.C.), the Greeks combined the Babylonian and Egyptian astrology with their own mathematics and astronomy, thereby forming the system presently used in the West.

In Ur of the Chaldeans, Sumerians may have brewed beer. Scientists say they have found the earliest known chemical evidence that ancient people drank beer: pale yellow deposits on the inside of a jar more than 5,000 years old. Tests suggested the deposits were calcium oxalate, a substance that settles out when beer was stored or fermented around 3,100 B.C.; archaeologists found several such sites in Mesopotamia. In an article in *Nature*, researchers stated that "the yellow deposits found in the grooves may have been put there to remove the bitter-tasting calcium oxalate from beer" (McGovern et al., 1992, p. 24).

Ur of the Chaldeans, south of Mesopotamia is the traditional birthplace of Abraham in the Delta of the Tigris and Euphrates Rivers (according to the Book of Genesis). Abraham is the Father of Judaism, Christianity, and Islam, which according to a 2017 Pew Research Center Survey comprise over half (54.6%) of today's world population (Pew Research Center, (2017, The Changing Religious

Global Landscape).

We read the following in Gen. 11:27-31: "This is the record of Terah. Terah became the father of Abraham, Nahor, and Haran. Haran died before his father Terah, in his native land, the Ur of the Chaldeans. Terah took his son Abraham and his daughter in law Sarai and brought them out of Ur of the Chaldeans to go to the land of Canaan." Then in Gen. 12:1 we read, "The lord God called Abraham saying: Go forth from your father's kinfolk and from your father's house to the land I will show you." In Gen. 15:7 the Lord said to Abraham: "I am the Lord who brought you from Ur of the Chaldeans to give you this land." St. Matthew's Gospel (1:1) gives the family record of Jesus Christ that he was descended from Abraham, a citizen of Ur of the Chaldeans.

Euphrates River

# Chapter II
# Chaldean Empire - Neo - Babylonians
## The Last Mesopotamian Monarchy (626-539 B.C.)

Around the ninth century B.C., history mentions a country called Chaldea with inhabitants called Chaldeans. This reference came from the reign of the Assyrian King Shalmanassar III (850 B.C.). Shalmanassar had come to the aid of his ally Babylon against the Aramaeans, where he encountered among others, the Chaldeans. This is the first mention of the people who were to play a leading role in history.

Chaldea, as a country, was mentioned in the Annals of the Assyrian King Ashurnasirpal II (884-859 B.C.). Before this time, the geographical area was called "Sea Lands." King Shalmanassar III (858-842 B.C.) of Assyria raided the area around 850 B.C. and reached the Persian Gulf. He called the country the *"Sea of Chaldea."*

By the end of the 12th century B.C., the 24th Dynasty of Kassites had ended in Mesopotamia. There followed a period of confusion. While the Assyrians were normally in control of Babylonia, the Aramaeans (a Semitic people) also attempted to seize power. Finally, the native leaders of Babylonia (Chaldeans) conquered the Assyrians and laid claim to power in Babylon.

These Chaldeans lived among the swamps and lakes along the lower courses of the Tigris and Euphrates Rivers. Their organization was tribal, and each Chaldean Baita (House, Family, and Clan) was under the leadership of a Malka (king). The political strength of each individual Malka was largely a matter of personal ability and prestige. The largest of the tribes, the Baith Dakuri, was located south of Borssipa, not far from Babylon.

Further south was the Baith Amukani, and along the Tigris to the east bordering Elan, was Baith Yakin. Chaldean tribes lived in an area of flourishing date palms. They kept large herds of horses and cattle; they were merchants in control of southern trade routes along which traveled such exotic luxuries as ebony, ivory, elephant hides, and gold.

The Chaldeans established a number of states which resisted extinction and assimilation during the Assyrian conquest of the eighth–seventh centuries B.C.

Little is known of the first Chaldean King of Babylon, who was succeeded by another Sea Land Malka, Eriba Marduk (770 B.C.). He seemed to have had some success in ridding the immediate neighborhood of Babylon and Borssipa of the ever-encroaching Aramaeans. Eriba Marduk is remembered by later Chaldean Kings as the true founder of their dynastic line. He was succeeded by Nabonassir in 747 B.C.

At this time, we enter a new era in the history of Babylon. Henceforth, precise records of historical events were systematically kept. These chronicles were an account of the succession of the Kings of Babylon. They also contained many accounts of astronomical observations. This is why the Nabonassir Era is recognized as a turning point in the history of science. In fact, the very term Chaldean became synonymous with astronomy. After the death of Nabonassir, a rebellion occurred in Babylon, which led to the murder of his son and the takeover by the Assyrian army.

Following the death of the Assyrian king Shalmanassir, a Chaldean Malka, the Ruler of the Family of Baith Yakin, came to power in Babylon (Read Isaiah. 39:1-2; 2 Kings 20:12-13). Merodach Baladan (721 B.C.) seized the Babylonian throne in 721 B.C., and held it until 710 B.C. (Read 2 Kings 20:12-13; 2 Chron. 32:31). Merodach Baladan was forced to flee to the marshes, where he was reinstated as King of the Baith Yakin Clan, leaving Babylon under the control of Assyrian officials.

Around the year 700 B.C. Ben Ibri, another Chaldean, attempted to come to power in Babylon. Seven years later, Mushezib Marduk tried to regain independence from the Assyrians, but he fled by sea and died there.

By the end of the first half of the seventh century B.C., a mysterious ruler by the name of Chaldalanu appeared as King of Babylon (649-

627 B.C.). Throughout all of this period, the Chaldeans remained strong, creating a threat to Assyrian power, which was nearing the point of collapse.

A Chaldean Malka named Nabupolassar seized the throne of Babylon. He established a wealthy and politically stable Chaldean Empire, which for the next eighty years was the principal power in Western Asia.

## The Six Chaldean Kings
### 1- Nabupolassar I (626 – 605 B.C.)

During the time of Ashurbanipal, King of Assyria (668-626), a Chaldean named Nabupolassar II founded the 31st Babylonian Dynasty from the Town of Uruk. He led a revolt against the Assyrians. He first drove them out of Uruk, then out of Babylon itself by the year 626 B.C.

He was the first Chaldean King to regain absolute independence from Babylon. A descendent of Merodach Baladan, Nabupolassar became a ruler of great power and influence. He joined his forces with those of the Median King Cyaxares and, in 612 B.C., took Nineveh and then Haran.

The last Assyrian outpost fell in 609 B.C. at which time the last Assyrian King, Assur Ubalit II (611- 609 B.C.), fled to the south to await his Egyptian allies. Egyptian troops under the command of Pharaoh Necho II joined the remnants of the Assyrian army at Carchemish. The crowned Prince Nebuchadnezzar II attacked in the spring of 605 B.C. While casualties were heavy on both sides (Jeremiah 46:12), the Egyptian forces were decisively defeated. Their troops bolted in disorder, pursued through Syria by the Chaldean army. Nabupolassar I died in Babylon on September 7, 605 B.C. News of his father's death reached Nebuchadnezzar II at Pelusium. Within a fortnight, he returned from the Egyptian border to Babylon where he assumed control.

## 2- Nebuchadnezzar II (604- 562 B.C.)

*(In Akkadian Language: Nabu- Apil- Usur: "god Nabu protector of the son").*

Nabupolassar named his oldest son after the famous King of the Second Dynasty of Isin who had died in 1126 B.C. Nebuchadnezzar II was to become the most famous king of the Neo-Babylonian Empire. He continued the extensive building projects of his father. By the year 605 B.C., he had gained control of all Syria and Palestine (Jeremiah 46:2-6).

In the same year, he also severely defeated the Egyptian army at Hama. The city of Ashkelon was conquered by Nebuchadnezzar II in 605 B.C., as well as a part of Judah. In the latter part of 601 B.C., he invaded Egypt and then returned to Babylon. Following his victory in Northern Arabia in the winter of 598 B.C., he personally led his army against Jerusalem. In 597 B.C., the city fell to him, and its king, Jehoiachin, was deported to Babylon with his court and many of the leading residents of the town. Nebuchadnezzar II then put Mattaniah in charge of Jerusalem in 590 B.C. Mattaniah led a revolt against Nebuchadnezzar II and was killed. Jerusalem itself was destroyed, following a bitter siege (589-578 B.C.).

The destruction of Jerusalem is recorded in Scripture (2 Kings 24:6-15; 2 Chronicles 36:9-10; Jeremiah 22:24-30; 27:20). The Temple of Jerusalem was looted, ten thousand captives were taken, and the nobles, craftsmen, and the royal household were deported to Babylon.

According to Jeremiah (25:27-29), Nebuchadnezzar II's success came from God himself so nothing could stop him. (See also: Jeremiah 32:1-5; 37:1-11; 38:14-23). This prophet mentions three deportations of the tribe of Judah by Nebuchadnezzar II: The first was in 598 B.C; he deported 3,023 people; the second in 587 B.C., deported 832 people; the third in 582 B.C., deported 755 people, bringing the total of deported people to 4,610. As the caravan route from Jerusalem to Babylon was 950 miles long, this great abduction of the citizenry of Jerusalem must have been a very organized affair. The prophet

Ezekiel (21:24) described Nebuchadnezzar II as casting lots at Reblah with God Himself directing the lot to Jerusalem.

According to the Book of Daniel, however, Nebuchadnezzar II was God's adversary (Daniel 1-4). Since there is no independent support for Nebuchadnezzar II's seven years of madness, the story is probably a later and fanciful interpretation of certain texts concerned with the eccentric Nabonidus, the last Chaldean king who deserted Babylon for a decade to live in Teima in Arabia (545 B.C.).

For thirteen years (585-573 B.C.), Nebuchadnezzar II laid unsuccessful siege to the city of Tyre. His campaign against Egypt (572-569 B.C.) was far more successful. Pharoah Hophra was defeated and dethroned, and from 569-536 B.C., the Babylonian army occupied Egypt.

Nebuchadnezzar II conquered Lebanon where he had an inscribed relief set up at Wadi Brissa not far from the river Alkalb. This relief shows Nebuchadnezzar II fighting a lion. The inscription makes mention of his care for the people of Lebanon.

History identifies Nebuchadnezzar II as the builder of the great and magnificent city of Babylon with its rose-colored walls, wide processional streets, and blue glazed bricks adorned with red dragons, lions, and wild bulls. He built a great defensive wall north of the city, which ran from Sippar to Opis (the famous Median Wall). This wall, designed to keep out barbarian invaders, was over 100 feet high. Not far from the temple, Nebuchadnezzar II built The Hanging Garden of Babylon. An artificial hill, it is said, was built for the love of his wife, Amytis, the daughter of the king of Medes, who came from the mountain county and found it hard to adjust to the plains of Mesopotamia. Irrigated pleasure gardens and groves were laid out along these terraces. As the water used for irrigation evaporated, it absorbed the heat from the caves that had been hollowed out under the terraces; thus, the caves could be used for cold storage.

Nebuchadnezzar II not only restored the city of Babylon, making it one of the wonders of the world, but also dug canals, built lakes and a great reservoir surrounding the city. For building materials, he used fired bricks mortared with asphalt and mud. Later, lime was substituted for mortar. Along with beautifying the royal residence, he finished the Tower of the Seven Planers of Borsippa.

Nebuchadnezzar II died in 562 B.C. after having built a Chaldean Empire, which extended from the Mediterranean Sea to the Persian Gulf.

### 3- Awil Merodach or "Evil Merodach" (561-560 B.C.):
(In Akkadian "Man of Marduk")

Merodach succeeded his father Nebuchadnezzar II, but his reign was short lived. He was driven from his throne and assassinated by his brother-in-law Neriglissar.

Little is known about Awil Merodach beyond his unpopularity with the priests of Babylon. He seemed to have shown leniency to Jehoiachim, the exiled King of Judea, releasing him from confinement, elevating him above the other captive kings, and admitting him to dine at the royal table (2 Kings 25:27; Jeremiah 52:31).

### 4- Nerigilssar (Nergal-Sharra-USAR) (560-556 B.C.)

According to the Book of Jeremiah (39:3-13), Neriglissar's son, Labashi-Marduk, a mere child, was murdered. Little is known of his reign beyond the fact that he restored the Temples of Babylon and Borssippa. He also undertook a campaign in 557 B.C. against Cilicia. Neriglissar died in 556 B.C. under questionable circumstances.

### 5- Labashi-Marduk (556 B.C.)

Labashi was the son of Nerigilissar and ascended the throne at a young age. Labashi was assassinated after just three months of rule.

### 6- Nabonidus (555-539 B.C.)

Nabonidus was the last king of an independent Babylon. A religious fanatic of Aramaean origin from Haran, Nabonidus was in his sixties before he ascended the throne of Babylon. He seemed to have been strongly influenced by his mother Adda-Guppi, a priestess of the temple of the god "Sin" at Haran. This influence caused him to replace the worship of Marduk and Nabu with the moon god, Sin.

Due to conflict with the priests in Babylon, Nabonidus moved his residence to northern Arabia. Having laid siege to Al-Jauf, 280 miles east of Akaba, he settled in Teima, the large oasis in Western Arabia. From there, he could easily wander from oasis to oasis as far as Yathrib (Al Madina). For ten years, Nabonidus stayed away from the capital city of Babylon. During this time, he left the government in the hands of his son Belshazzar, a capable soldier, but a poor politician. Belshazzar's authority was challenged by the increasing influence of the Persians.

At the age of seventy, Nabonidus returned to Babylon, but his career was short-lived. The priest of Marduk, in Babylon, sided with the Persian leader Cyrus, with whom they enjoyed better relations. Cyrus attacked Babylon in the Autumn of 539 B.C. He defeated Nabonidus and entered the city of Babylon without as much as a skirmish. For his surrender, Nabonidus received a small territory in Persia.

Nabonidus' surrender marked the end of the last native ruling Dynasty in Babylon. The rule of the Chaldean Kings, however, has left a profound mark on the history for this area. Inscriptions on the monuments, letters, and legal and commercial documents in great number have helped us to form a complete picture of life in the Neo-Babylonian (Chaldean) Empire. Perhaps the prophet Jeremiah (51:7) best summed up Chaldean rule in his description of Babylon of the Chaldeans as *"...a golden cup in the Lord's hand that made all the earth drunk."* Also, the prophet Habakkuk (1:6-11) described the Chaldeans as *"Thus said the Lord. I am raising up Chaldeans, the people that march the breadth of the land... Swifter than leopards are their horses and keener than wolves at evening. Their horses prance, their horsemen come from afar: They fly like the eagle hastening to devour; each comes from the rapine, their combined onset is that of a storm wind that heaps up captives like sand. They scoff at Kings, and princes are their laughing stock; they laugh at any fortress, they heap up a ramp and conquer it. Then they veer like the wind and they are gone."*

After the fall of Babylon to the Persians, many attempts were made by Chaldeans to return to power, but none was successful. Historians record three major rebellions led by Chaldeans: The first rebellion occurred in 522-521 B.C. when Nidunta-Bel or Nebuchadnezzar III seized the throne in Babylon. He was killed shortly thereafter, and the movement failed. The second rebellion occurred in 521 B.C. when the Chaldean general, Nebuchadnezzar IV, led an unsuccessful revolt and was put to death. The third rebellion was when the last Chaldeans to make an effort to regain power in Babylon, Bel-Shimanni and Shamseh-Eribe, led a rebellion in 482 B.C., but were both killed. After this time, the Chaldeans continued to roam Mesopotamia with their brothers, the Assyrians. Both represented a civilization already thousands of years old.

The fall of Nineveh in 612 B.C. and Babylon in 539 B.C. marked the decline of Mesopotamian civilization and the end of the last native ruling dynasty in Mesopotamia.

## The following foreign invaders dominated Mesopotamia in succession between 539 B.C.–1958 A.D.:

1- The **Achemenian** Persians 539–335 B.C.
2- The **Greeks** 331–130 B.C.
3- The **Parthians** 130 B.C.–226 A.D.
4- The **Sassanians** 226–636 A.D.
5- The **Mongols** 258–356 A.D.
6- The **Arabs** 636–1258 A.D.
7- The **Jalaired Dynasty** 1356–1410 A.D.
8- The **Turkmans** 1410–1509 A.D.
9- The **First Ottoman Turks period** 1534–1621 A.D.
10- The **Second Persians period** 1621–1638 A.D.
11- The **Second Ottoman Turks period** 1638–1916 A.D.
12- The **British**, under General Maude with the help of soldiers from India, captured the capital Baghdad in 1917.
13- **Arabian Kings** ruled in succession from 1921–1958 A.D.
14- **Iraq became a Republic in 1958 A.D.**

# Chapter III
# The Chaldean Church

Since the second half of the first century A.D., Christianity has flourished in Mesopotamia among the descendants of the two great and ancient nations of Chaldea and Assyria. Once they were baptized, both nations preferred the name Christian to their old national names. This church was comprised of these two nations, and because the church was located east of the Roman Empire and separated by the Euphrates River, it was simply called, "The Church of the East." The Church in Mesopotamia prospered and expanded into the whole of Chaldea, Assyria, Persia, Arabia, the steppes of Mongolia in Asia, the Malabar Coast of India, and even into China. During the first five centuries A.D., the Chaldean and Assyrian Church were one in faith with the Roman Catholic Church.

A school for Christian learning was even established in Edessa (modern Urfa). This school reached its highest glory under Mar Aprem (St. Ephrem) in 363 A.D. However, the Church of the East separated from Rome around the Council of Mar Dadeesho in 424 A.D. The Church of the East fathers declared that the new head of the Church of the East was the final authority.

The head of the newly independent Church of the East in Mesopotamia was given the title, "Cathilikos" meaning the common father or the whole. In 424 A.D., the Council of Dadishua declared that the Church of the East is the last reference for the Church. The Cathilikos resided in Seleucia - Cteisphon, near Baghdad, Iraq. In the seventh century, Mesopotamia was conquered by the Moslems. In 780 A.D., the Cathilikos Timetheos moved his residence to the new capital of Baghdad.

By the end of the tenth century A.D., there were fifteen metropolitan church provinces in Mesopotamia, and five beyond its border, including those in Iran, Syria, Egypt, India, and China. These church provinces even extended into eastern Siberia and Mongolia.

An attempt on the part of the Church of the East in Mesopotamia to be reunited with the Catholic Church was realized when the Patriarch John Sulaka went to Rome and made his profession of the Catholic Faith before Pope Julius III in 1553. By 1592, however, most Mesopotamian Catholics had separated again from Rome. Periodically, various groups of them had reunited with Rome only to break ties again after a few years. By the nineteenth century, reunited Catholics outnumbered those who were not united, though some were still separate.

Chaldeans, as a nation, existed since the seventh century B.C. Today's Chaldeans are descendants of that great nation. The term "Chaldean Church" was in popular use, and in 1445 A.D. Pope Euginius V utilized this term to distinguish the followers of the Church of the East of Cyprus, who were newly reconciled with Rome, from those who had not reconciled. We can observe that when converts from the Church of the East who emigrated to Cyprus declared their Chaldean identity, the Latin Church respected their Chaldean identity by keeping their original Chaldean name.

It is important to note that the Chaldean people were spread out, living in Iraq and the Middle East for thousands of years. When the pope recognized a small community of Chaldeans living in Cyprus as the "Chaldean Church," he did not create a name for them but rather confirmed and proclaimed their origin and acknowledged that the last native Mesopotamian rulers were the Chaldeans and, since their fall to the Persians in 539 B.C., Iraq was ruled by foreigners. Thus, the Chaldeans remain as the original people of Iraq, contrary to the claim of some who believe that the name, "Chaldean" appeared in the fifteenth century A.D. The fact that a small number of Chaldeans living as a community in Cyprus was called the Chaldean Church in the fifteenth century, did not nullify the existence of the Chaldeans prior to that or throughout the church history.

Modern Wall in Babylon with Cross

# Chapter IV
# The Chaldean Church in the World

The Chaldean Church consists of Middle Eastern Christians who use Aramaic as their mother tongue. It is one of the twenty-two Eastern Rite Churches recognized by the Holy See of Rome. Chaldeans are Catholics in union with Rome, but they are not Roman Catholics. Chaldean Catholics are one in faith with Rome, but different in customs (rites). Their liturgy is different, though Chaldean Catholics have the same sacraments. They baptize and confirm infants. Some Chaldean Catholic priests are married, though most priests embrace optional celibacy. Chaldean Catholics have their own bishops, which form a hierarchy independent of Roman bishops. However, the patriarch who leads the Chaldean Church is under jurisdiction of the Pope.

The Chaldean Patriarch used to be called the Patriarch of Babylon, but in an August 2021 meeting of Chaldean Bishops, his title was changed to the, "Patriarch of Chaldeans." The Patriarch of Chaldeans resides in Baghdad, Iraq. The Patriarch's flock of Chaldeans are scattered throughout the world and are estimated at several million, of which 500,000 reside in Iraq, around 250,000 in the U.S., and the rest spread throughout the world.

According to the 2008 Church Census, there are eight Chaldean Archdioceses and nine Dioceses, with eighteen Bishops. There are around one hundred and twelve parishes and ten missions served by about one hundred and ten priests. Since 2003, Chaldean Catholics have been persecuted in Iraq, especially in Baghdad and Mosul. Many clerics were martyred and many parishes are semi-closed, forcing their pastors to leave to other cities in the north of Iraq or leave the country seeking refuge in any country offering them haven. There is one religious order near Alqosh, Iraq, of men consisting of approximately forty monks and one seminary with around fifty theology and philosophy students preparing for the priesthood. There are two orders of religious women in Baghdad, the Chaldean Daughters of Mary Immaculate and the Sacred Heart Chaldean Sisters.

Your cross saved us. Your cross saves us.
Let your cross be a wall for ourselves

# Chapter V
# The Chaldean Church in the United States

The first pioneers of the Chaldean people arrived to the United States at the end of the nineteenth century. They were few in number, but by the mid-twentieth century, there were many spread all over the country.

As of July 25, 2002, Chaldeans in the U.S. have two dioceses; one includes the Eastern States, and the other includes the Western States. These dioceses are also known as Eparchies, which is a term used to refer to Dioceses of Eastern Rite Chaldean Churches.

The first diocese or eparchy is St. Thomas the Apostle and is based in Metropolitan Detroit, Michigan. It covers thirty-one states with more than a hundred and twenty thousand members in twelve parishes, ten of which are in the Detroit area, and two of which are in the Chicago area. The twelve parishes are:

1- *Our Lady of Chaldeans Cathedral* (Southfield, Michigan)

2- *Sacred Heart* (Detroit, Michigan)

3- *Mar Addai* (Oak Park, Michigan)

4- *St. Joseph* (Troy, Michigan)

5- *St. Thomas* (West Bloomfield, Michigan)

6- *Saint George Church* (Shelby Township, Michigan)

7- *Holy Martyrs* (Sterling Heights, Michigan)

8- *Our Lady of Perpetual Help* (Warren, Michigan)

9- *Holy Cross* (Farmington Hills, Michigan)

10- *St. Paul* (Grant Blanc, Michigan)

11- *St. Ephrem* (Chicago, Illinois)

12- *Mart Maryam* (Chicago, Illinois)

The second diocese or eparchy is St. Peter the Apostle of the Chaldeans and is based in San Diego, California. It covers nineteen states with more than forty thousand members in eleven parishes and three missions. The eleven parishes are:

1- *St. Peter Cathedral* (El Cajon, California)
2- *St. Michael* (El Cajon, California)
3- *St. Paul* (North Hollywood, California)
4- *St. George* (Santa Ana, California)
5- *St. Thomas* (Turlock, California)
6- *St. Mary* (Campbell, California)
7- *Mar Awraha* (Scottsdale, Arizona)
8- *Santa Barbara* (Las Vegas, Nevada)
9- *Saint Matthew's Assyrian Chaldean Catholic Church* (Ceres, California)
10- *Our Lady of Perpetual Help* (Sacramento, California)
11- *St. John the Apostle* (El Cajon, California)

**On January 26, 1982:** His Holiness John Paul II established an apostolic exarchate for the Chaldean faithful who are residents of the United States, and he appointed Rev. Ibrahim Ibrahim as the First Apostolic Exarch on March 7, 1982. On April 18 of that year, Rev. Ibrahim was ordained Bishop in Baghdad and was installed as the first bishop of the new exarchate. Pope John Paul II elevated the apostolic exarchate of the Chaldeans of the United States to the rank of eparchy (diocese) on August 3, 1985. The official title of this diocese was The Chaldean Diocese of St. Thomas the Apostle. His Excellency Mar Ibrahim Ibrahim resided in Detroit, and the seat of his Diocese was Our Lady of Chaldeans Catholic Cathedral.

**On May 21, 2002:** St. Peter's Chaldean Catholic Church in El Cajon, California, became the seat of the second Chaldean diocese in the United States. It is now called St. Peter's Chaldean Catholic Cathedral.

The new diocese was established by Pope John Paul II at the request of the bishops of the Chaldean Church and includes the following nineteen States: Arizona, Alaska, California, Colorado, Hawaii, Idaho, Kansas, Montana, Nebraska, Nevada, Oklahoma, New Mexico, North Dakota, South Dakota, Oregon, Texas, Utah,

Washington, and Wyoming.

The Holy Father appointed a Chaldean priest named Rev. Sarhad Yawsip Jammo as the first bishop of the newly established diocese. Bishop Sarhad Yawsip was born in Baghdad, Iraq, in 1941. Fr. Yawsip was ordained a Chaldean priest in Rome in 1964. Fr. Yawsip then returned to Baghdad, where he served as a pastor and then the rector at St. Peter's Chaldean Seminary. Fr. Yawsip moved to the United States in 1977 to serve the Chaldeans of Michigan, where he remained until he was ordained a bishop on July 18, 2002 in Troy, Michigan. On July 25, 2002 Bishop Sarhad Yawsip was installed at St. Peter's Chaldean Catholic Cathedral in San Diego, California.

**Jan. 15, 2008:** Joining the Chaldean Catholic Church:

Between the months of January and May 2008, Bishop Mar Bawai Soro, along with 6 priests, 30 deacons and 5,000 faithful (formerly belonging to the Assyrian Church of the East) officially joined the Chaldean Catholic Church.

# Chapter VI
# The Chaldean Catholic Community In San Diego

A great majority of San Diego Chaldeans trace their roots to the province of Nineveh in northern Mesopotamia (Iraq). These Chaldeans left their country searching for a better life and hoping for a more peaceful and serene atmosphere.

According to the recent statistics of St. Peter's Cathedral, as of October 2009, the population consists of 2,457 families with 11,451 of our Chaldeans presently registered (this figure does not include those families or individuals who had not yet registered). In 2017, the approximate number of Chaldean Catholics in San Diego County is estimated to be 40,000.

The following are important historical stages of the emigration of Chaldeans either from Detroit, Michigan, or directly from Mesopotamia (Iraq) to San Diego.

**Dec. 1951:** The first-known Chaldean immigrant in San Diego was Dr. Joseph Gibran. who came for medical research. A trickle of immigrants followed over the next decade.

**Aug. 1954:** Mr. Ramzi Alex Thomas arrived from Baghdad to study at San Diego State University. After he completed his studies, he opened his own business, Used Auto Parts Sales.

**June 1955:** Mr. and Mrs. Aziz Habib visited San Diego for two weeks from Detroit. In July 1957, they moved to San Diego. They were the first Chaldeans to open a grocery store.

**June 1959:** Mr. and Mrs. Wadie Deddeh moved to Chula Vista in San Diego from Detroit. Born in Iraq, Wadie Deddeh moved to Detroit in the 1940s where he studied constitutional law and political science and married Mary-Lynn Drake. Their son, Peter, became Presiding Judge of the San Diego Superior Court.

Wadie P. Deddeh first became a political science teacher at a community college. Later Wadie Deddeh served in the California Assembly from 1967 to 1983 and in the State Senate from 1983 to 1993.

Senator Deddeh, a Democrat, joined President John F. Kennedy's campaign. He served in the California State Legislature for over 25 years, later running (unsuccessfully) for Congress.

In Sacramento, Deddeh served for many years on the Revenue and Taxation Committee. He died at the age of 98 years old, Aug. 30, 2019. A state office building was named after Deddeh, who was known as the Father of Caltrans.

**June 1960:** Mr. Slewa Semaan arrived from Baghdad to visit San Diego. He found about 10 Chaldean families living here.

**Dec. 06, 1973:** The first Chaldean Catholic Parish was established and Rev. Peter J. Kattoula, a Chaldean priest, was assigned as its pastor. At that time, there were 70 Chaldean families in San Diego.

**March 25, 1974:** According to the first private census of St. Peter's Parish, the population consisted of 117 Chaldean families (this figure does not include those families or individuals who had not yet registered).

**April 1974:** The Pastor and the Parish Council decided to name this newly established Parish, St. Peter's Chaldean Catholic Parish in San Diego.

**May 20, 1974:** St. Peter's Parish purchased 5.09 acres of land for $48,355 near Rancho San Diego: the present site of the church. The final payment for this land was made on June 10, 1979 and reached a total of $56,442. From 1983 to 2003, the Parish expanded to include St. Peter's Church, a social and religious hall, the Old Rectory, and the New Rectory.

**June 20, 1974:** Fr. Michael J. Bazzi arrived from Rome to visit San Diego. At that time, the population of St. Peter's Parish consisted of 130 registered families.

**April 15, 1975:** St. Peter Parish published its first directory. The population then consisted of 150 registered Chaldean families in San Diego.

**June 29, 1977:** St. Peter's Parish population consisted of 220 Chaldean families with a total of 950 parishioners (this figure does not include those families or individuals who had not yet registered).

**Oct. 09, 1978:** Rev. Ibrahim Ibrahim (currently the Bishop Emeritus of St. Thomas Diocese) arrived from Baghdad to assist at St. Peter's Parish. He served with the pastor, Fr. Peter Kattoula, from Oct. 19, 1978 to Jan. 1, 1979, after which he left for Los Angeles to establish a new Chaldean Parish.

**June 29, 1979:** St. Peter's Parish celebrated the ground breaking for the new church. On the same day, the Parish published the second edition of its directory. The population of St. Peter's Parish in San Diego consisted of 300 registered Chaldean families with a total of 1,190 parishioners. After two weeks, Fr. Peter Kattoula placed a metal cylinder into a small trench in the foundation under the altar in the presence of Mr. Najib Sesi, President of the Parish Council. Inside the capsule is the story of how our growing Chaldean community raised the money for the construction of the church.

**Nov. 27, 1981:** Two Chaldean Sisters, daughters of Mary the Immaculate Conception in Baghdad, Iraq, arrived to serve St. Peter's Parish.

**Jan. 26, 1982:** His holiness John Paul II established St. Thomas Exarchate on March 7, 1982 and Rev. Ibrahim Ibrahim was installed as the first Bishop of the new exarchate. Pope John Paul II elevated apostolic exarchate of the Chaldeans of the United States to the rank of Eparchy (Diocese) on August 3, 1985. St. Peter's Parish was part of the diocese until May 21, 2002, when St. Peter's Chaldean Catholic Church in El Cajon, California, became the seat of the second Chaldean Diocese of St. Peter the Apostle in the United States, besides St. Thomas Eparchy.

**May 05, 1982 - Sept. 30, 1982:** The Rectory – Old Priest House was constructed.

**Nov. 8, 1982 - June 29, 1984:** St. Peter's Church was constructed.

**Jan. 05, 1983:** St. Peter's Chaldean Catholic parish population consisted of 411 registered families.

**Sept. 10, 1983:** St. Peter's Church building was dedicated according to the Chaldean Eastern Catholic rite.

**Jan. 05, 1984:** St. Peter's Chaldean Catholic parish population consisted of 495 registered families.

**Sept. 1, 1985:** Fr. Michael J. Bazzi was assigned to assist at St. Peter's Parish. On April 25, 1986, Bishop Ibrahim Ibrahim granted Fr. Bazzi the faculty of Pastor to serve with Rev. Kattoula.

**Dec. 10, 1985:** St. Peter's Parish Census recorded 549 Chaldean families, with a total of 2,054 registered parishioners

**Jan. 10, 1986:** The following activities were established at St. Peter's Church: Bible Study (40 members), College Students and Graduates Bible Study (53 members), Choir (15 members); Catechism School: Preschool through Eighth Grade (270 students taught by 18 teachers), High School Class (30 students), and a Classical Aramaic Study (16 students). An English Choir, with 12 members, started in 1987. Sacred Heart Sodality was also established in 1987 with 55 members. These activities were established by Fr. Michael J. Bazzi after three months of his assignment at St. Peter's Parish.

**Nov. 05, 1986:** The registered Chaldeans were divided geographically throughout San Diego as follows:

| City | Number of people | Number of families | Number of singles |
|---|---|---|---|
| El Cajon | 1,377 | 291 | 27 |
| Spring Valley | 436 | 87 | 6 |
| La Mesa | 259 | 57 | 5 |
| San Diego | 181 | 39 | 5 |
| Chula Vista | 77 | 17 | 2 |
| Santee | 70 | 13 | 1 |
| Bonita | 52 | 12 | 0 |
| Lakeside | 14 | 3 | 0 |
| Escondido | 11 | 2 | 0 |
| Lemon Grove | 5 | 1 | 2 |
| Other Cities | 76 | 17 | 2 |
| **Total** | **2,558** | **539** | **46** |

(This figure does not include those families or individuals who had not yet registered)

**March 20, 1987:** Rev. Peter Kattoula passed away. He established St. Peter's Parish and served the Chaldean Community of San Diego as a Pastor for 14 years.

**March 27, 1987:** Fr. Michael J. Bazzi was installed as Pastor of St. Peter's Parish.

**Dec. 15, 1987:** St. Peter's Chaldean Catholic Parish population consisted of 600 families with a total of 3,000 registered parishioners.

**Jan. 25, 1988:** St. Peter's Parish statistics indicate that there are 800 registered Chaldean families with a total of 4,000 parishioners

**Jan. 28, 1988 – Sept. 30, 1989:** At this time, construction continued in building St. Peter's Church Hall, which was officially dedicated on Nov. 29, 1989.

**Nov. 15, 1989:** According to the new St. Peter's Parish Directory, the number of registered families was 740. There were 382 families with one business and 50 families with two or more businesses.

**Oct. 03, 1993:** St. Peter's Parish population consisted of 1,078 registered families with a total of 4,964 parishioners.

**Sept. 15, 1994:** St. Peter's population consisted of 1,197 families with a total of 5,571 parishioners (this figure does not include those families or individuals who have not yet registered).

**Nov. 15, 1996:** The total number of registered families was 1,335 (this figure does not include those families or individuals who have not yet registered). There were 689 families with one business and 102 families with two or more businesses.

**June, 1998:** Judge Peter C. Deddeh was appointed to the California Superior Court, County of San Diego, by Governor Pete Wilson. Judge Deddeh was the East County Branch Supervising Judge of the El Cajon Superior Court (2007-2011), Presiding Judge of the Appellate Panel (2007), Criminal Presiding Judge for San Diego Superior Court (2001-2005) and for Vista Superior Court (1998-2000).

In addition to Judge Deddeh's work in Criminal, he presided over Homeless Court sessions at St. Vincent De Paul Village and the Vietnam Veterans of San Diego Homeless Shelter. Before joining the Superior Court bench, Deddeh was Deputy District Attorney (1993-

1998) prosecuting felony and misdemeanor crimes committed from National City south to the Mexican border, felony and misdemeanor crimes committed by juveniles in San Diego County, and street gang members for violent felony offenses.

Peter Deddeh is a graduate of the University of California, Santa Barbara (BA, History/Political Science, 1978), and University of San Diego School of Law (JD, 1982). Judge Deddeh's term ends on January 6, 2025.

**Oct. 03, 1999:** St. Peter's Parish records indicated that there are 1,821 registered Chaldean families with a total of 9,105 parishioners.

**Oct. 06, 1999:** St. Michael's Church was dedicated and Fr. Sabri Kejbo was assigned as the first Pastor of the second Parish for Chaldeans in El Cajon under the name of St. Michael's Chaldean Catholic Church.

**May 21, 2002:** St. Peter's Chaldean Catholic Church in El Cajon, California, became the seat of the second Chaldean Diocese in the United States. It was called St. Peter's Chaldean Catholic Cathedral.

The Holy Father, Pope John Paul II, created a second diocese for the Chaldean Church in the United States. The new diocese would divide the country between the east and west. Mar Sarhad Jammo would be given an apostolic seat to preside over the Eparchy of St. Peter the Apostle covering the western United States. Pope John II appointed a Chaldean Priest, Rev. Sarhad Yawsip Jammo, as the first Bishop of the newly established diocese. Bishop Jammo was installed July 25, 2002. His term ended May 07, 2016.

Mar Sarhad Yawsip Hermiz Jammo was born on March 14, 1941, in Baghdad, Iraq. He entered St. Peter's seminary in Mosul and left for Rome at the age of 17. Jammo attended the Pontifical Urbaniana University, where he earned Master's degrees in philosophy and theology. Jammo was ordained a priest on Dec.19, 1964. Jammo pursued doctoral studies at the Pontifical Oriental Institute, where he earned a Ph.D. in Eastern Ecclesiastical Studies. Dr. Jammo's dissertation was titled, "The Structure of the Chaldean Mass." Dr. Jammo taught at the Pontifical Oriental Institute after finishing his studies in Rome.

Rev. Jammo was appointed pastor of St. John the Baptist Parish in Baghdad, where he would serve from 1969 to 1974. During this time, he became the rector at the Chaldean Patriarchal Seminary. In 1977, Rev. Jammo was made associate pastor of Mother of God parish in Southfield, Michigan, USA. In 1983, Rev. Jammo was appointed pastor of St. Joseph's Church in Troy, Michigan, in which capacity he would serve until his elevation to the episcopacy.

Rev. Jammo was ordained bishop July 18, 2002, and was installed July 25, 2002.

**Jan. 17, 2003:** The new rectory of St. Peter's Chaldean Catholic Cathedral was dedicated.

**Jan. 15, 2004:** St. Peter's Parish records indicate that there were 2,075 registered Chaldean families

**Jan. 15, 2006:** St. Peter's Chaldean Catholic Cathedral population consisted of 2,267 registered families.

**Jan. 15, 2007:** St. Peter's Chaldean Catholic Cathedral population consisted of 2,610 registered families

**May 16, 2007:** His Excellency Mar Sarhad Yawsip Jammo, at St. Peter's Cathedral, accepted the temporary promises of three young girls, the founding members of the new Diocesan Lay Association named "Workers of the Vineyard" in El Cajon, California. In 2018, Workers of the Vineyard closed.

**Jan. 05, 2008:** St. Peter's Chaldean Catholic Cathedral population consisted of 2,856 registered families with a total of 7,383 parishioners

**July 23, 2008:** Mrs. Polly Haisha Shamoon, 42, became the first female Chaldean Judge in the State of California and was appointed to the San Diego County Superior Court.

**July 25, 2008:** The Seminary of Mar Abba the Great in El Cajon was dedicated by Mar Sarhad Yawsip Jammo. Five young men from St. Peter Cathedral enrolled in the new seminary.

**January 12, 2009:** Bishop Mar Bawai Soro moved to reside in San Diego at the Episcopal Residence with Bishop Mar Sarhad Yawsip Jammo.

**Jan. 16, 2009:** St Peter's Chaldean Catholic Cathedral celebrated the 35th Anniversary of St. Peter's Parish Establishment and the 25th Anniversary (Silver Jubilee) of St. Peter's Church Dedication.

St. Peter Diocesan Clergy

## Chaldeans in the San Diego Area As of Oct. 2009

The Chaldeans who are registered with the church are divided throughout San Diego County as follows:

| City | Number of Families | Population | Percentage |
|---|---|---|---|
| El Cajon | 1,452 | 7,260.00 | 64.39% |
| Spring Valley | 247 | 988 | 10.95% |
| San Diego | 140 | 560 | 6.21% |
| La Mesa | 122 | 488 | 5.41% |
| Jamul | 45 | 225 | 2.00% |
| Chula Vista | 32 | 128 | 1.42% |
| Lakeside | 32 | 160 | 1.42% |
| Escondido | 27 | 108 | 1.20% |
| Santee | 26 | 130 | 1.15% |
| Bonita | 16 | 80 | 0.71% |
| Oceanside | 9 | 45 | 0.40% |
| Vista | 9 | 36 | 0.40% |
| Carlsbad | 9 | 36 | 0.40% |
| Alpine | 7 | 28 | 0.31% |
| Poway | 7 | 35 | 0.31% |
| San Marcos | 6 | 24 | 0.27% |
| Other Cities | 280 | 1,120 | 12.44% |
| Total | 2,457 | 11,451 | |

**January 11, 2014:** Bishop Bawai Soro was appointed by Pope Francis to be the auxiliary Eparch for St. Peter Diocese and Titular Bishop of Fortiana.

**May 2014:** His Holiness, Pope Francis appointed Fr. Frank Kalabat as the new Bishop of the Chaldean Diocese of St. Thomas the Apostle. Bishop Kalabat succeeded Bishop Mar Ibrahim Ibrahim who submitted his resignation when he reached retirement age. Bishop

Mar Francis Kalabat was ordained on June 15, 2014, at Mother of God Cathedral in Detroit, Michigan.

**April 1, 2015:** New Chaldean Monastery – St. Joseph's Monastery - was established with one priest and two Monks. In February, 2021, the name of the monastery was changed from St. Joseph's to Sons of the Covenant Monastery.

**May 7, 2016:** The Holy Father accepted the resignation from the pastoral care of the eparchy of St. Peter the Apostle of San Diego of the Chaldeans, USA, presented by Bishop Sarhad Yawsip Jammo, and appointed Bishop Shlemon Warduni, auxiliary of Baghdad of the Chaldeans, as apostolic administrator.

**May 14, 2016:** Bishop Shlemon Warduni arrived to San Diego. Bishop Warduni was the Apostolic Administrator until the appointment of the second Eparch, Bishop Emanuel Shaleta.

**July 7, 2017:** A small third Church with twenty parking spaces was purchased in San Diego, St. John's Chaldean Catholic Church. The property and edifice were donated by a Chaldean family living in San Diego.

**August 9, 2017:** Pope Francis appointed H.E. Mar Emanuel Hana Shaleta as the new bishop of the Eparchy of St. Peter the Apostle of San Diego.

**August 25, 2017:** His Beatitude Patriarch Louis Sako arrived for his first pastoral visit to St. Peter Chaldean Catholic Diocese. The pastoral visit lasted until September 9, 2017.

**August 29, 2017:** Bishop Emanuel Hana Shaleta was installed as the second Eparch for the Chaldean Catholic Eparchy of St. Peter the Apostle by His Beatitude Patriarch Louis Sako at St. Peter Cathedral.

The Pope appointed as eparchial bishop of Saint Peter Apostle of San Diego, Msgr. Emanuel Hana Shaleta, transferring him from the Chaldean Catholic Eparchy of Mar Addai of Toronto, Canada.

Bishop H.E. Msgr. Emanuel Hana Shaleta was born in Fishkabour-Zakho, Iraq, on November 11, 1956. Following his primary studies in his village in 1971, Shaleta entered St. John's Minor Seminary run by the Dominicans, near Mosul. In 1977, Shaleta was sent to the Pontifical Urbanian University in Rome, where he carried out his studies in philosophy and theology.

Fr. Shaleta was ordained a priest by the laying on of hands by Pope St. John Paul II on 31 May 1984.

Rev. Shaleta continued his studies in theology of the Urbanian University and obtained a doctorate in Biblical Theology in 1987. Fr. Shaleta was transferred to the United States of America, where from 1987 to 2000, he served in the parish of St. Paul, North Hollywood, California. From 2000 to 2002, Fr. Shaleta was deputy priest of St. Joseph, Troy, Michigan, until 2006 when Fr. Shaleta became pastor. Fr. Shaleta next served as parish priest of St. George in Shelby Township, Michigan, until 2015.

**On January 15, 2015:** the Holy Father Pope Francis appointed Shaleta as Bishop of the Chaldean Catholic Eparchy of Mar Addai of Toronto, Canada. Bishop Shaleta was ordained on February 6, 2015. Shaleta was appointed Bishop of San Diego in 2017.

**October 31, 2017:** Bishop Bawai Soro was appointed by Pope Francis to be the Eparch for the Chaldean Catholic Eparchy of Mar Addai of Toronto, Canada.

St. Peter's Cathedral, El Cajon, California

# Chapter VII
# The Eastern Catholic Churches

Christianity in the early centuries spread rapidly throughout the ancient Middle East and Europe. The countries which were located east of the Mediterranean Sea had their own liturgies, which were celebrated in their local languages. The Fathers of the Church labeled those liturgies as Eastern Rites; while Rome, located west of the Mediterranean Sea, celebrated the liturgy according to the Western (Latin) Roman Rite.

The Catholic Church is a communion of Particular Churches of the East and of the West. These are known as "ritual churches sui iuris" (in Latin "of their own law" or "autonomous"), which refers to their legal status as having the capacity to govern themselves according to their own laws. Each of the Eastern Catholic Churches is an autonomous Church.

The Catholic Church currently contains twenty-three autonomous churches, which are primarily self-governing under the Roman Pontiff, with whom they are in full communion and in whom universal communion is realized.

**The following is a list of the Autonomous Catholic Churches, arranged according to the tradition they observe:**

**I. Alexandrian:** 1. Coptic, 2. Ethiopian.

**II. Antiochene:** 3. Malankar, 4. Maronite, 5. Syrian

**III. Constantinopolitan:** 6. Albanian, 7. Belorussian, 8. Bulgarian, 9. Greek, 10. Hungarian, 11. Italo-Albanian, 12. Melkite, 13. Romanian, 14. Russian, 15. Ruthenian, 16. Slovak, 17. Ukrainian, 18. Yugoslav, 19. Georgian

**IV. Armenian:** 20. Armenian

**V. Chaldean:** 21. Chaldean, 22. Malabar

**VI. Latin (Western):** 23. Roman

The major original Eastern Churches in the Roman Empire were: Rome, and later the Jerusalem, Antiochene, Alexandrian, Byzantine, Malabari, Armenian, and Chaldean Churches. Each of the Eastern Churches are divided into sub-divisions, which use, for the most part, their own language and have their own adaptations of law and liturgy. The Antiochene Rite uses Aramaic as its principal language. It receives its name from the town of Antioch in Syria, where for the first time, the followers of Christ were named Christians around the year A.D 40 (Acts 11:26).

The Eastern Churches include the Chaldean-Assyrian Catholic Church, using the Aramaic language, and the Malabrese Church. The Western Antiochian Churches contain the Syrian, Malankarese, and the Maronite Churches. The Alexandrian Church uses Coptic as its principal language for the celebration of its liturgies and is used by the Coptic and Ethiopic Churches. The Byzantine Church uses Greek as its principal language.

Today the ecclesial life of the Eastern Catholic Churches is Governed in accordance with the Code of Canons of the Eastern Churches (CCEO), which was promulgated by Pope John Paul II on October 18, 1990 and began to have force of law on October 1, 1991. According to the new Eastern Code, the Eastern Catholic Churches fall into four categories:

**I. Patriarchal:** Presided over by a Patriarch who has power over Metropolitans, Bishops, and other Christian faithful of his Church according to the form of law. The Patriarchal Churches are: 1. Chaldean Church, 2. Armenian Church, 3. Coptic Church, 4. Syrian Church, 5. Maronite Church, 6. Melkite Church.

**II. Major Archiepiscopal:** governed by a major archbishop. His power and those of the Synod of Bishops are equal to those of the patriarch and the Synod of Bishops of the patriarchal Church, respectively. These Churches include: 7. Ukrainian Church, 8. Malabar Church.

**III. Metropolitan Autonomous:** presided over by a Metropolitan, who is to be distinguished from metropolitan presiding over an ecclesiastical province of a Patriarchal Church of Major Archiepiscopal Church. These include: 9. Ethiopian Church, 10. Syro-Malankara Church, 11. American Ruthenian Church, 12. Romanian Church.

**IV. Other Autonomous Churches:** These Churches have the lowest degree of ecclesial autonomy, hardly higher than that of any other diocese/eparchy. The Churches with hierarchy are: 13. Bulgarian Church, 14. Greek Church, 15. Hungarian Church, 16. Italo-Albanian Church, 17. Slovak Church, 18. Yugoslav Church, and the Churches with no hierarchy are: 19. Belorussian Church, 20. Albanian Church, 21. Georgian Church, 22. Russian Church.

# Chapter VIII
# The Chaldean Rite

The Chaldean rite is used by the people whose homeland is Mesopotamia, Babylonia and Assyria. They received the Gospel message from St. Thomas the Apostle, St. Addai (possibly Thaddeus, one of the twelve apostles), and two of Addai's disciples, Sts. Aggai and Mari. Sts. Addai and Mari are credited with establishing the first liturgical forms.

## The Liturgical Year According to the Chaldean Eastern Rite

The liturgical cycle used by Chaldeans today was arranged in the 7th century A.D. during the patriarchate of Esho'yab Hdhayawaya. The cycle reflects the plan of God for the salvation of humankind, from the Annunciation (of Christ's birth) through Parousia (the second coming of Christ.) It is divided into several seasons of shawo'eh.

Most shawo'eh consist of seven weeks. Some have a fixed number of weeks and never change, while others vary from year to year. The first and the last shawo'eh always consist of four weeks. The Chaldean Mass is very ancient and originated around the second century A.D. based on the liturgies celebrated by St. Thomas the Apostle, Mar Addai, and Mar Mari. The Aramaic language is used as its principal language.

# The Chaldean Liturgical (Cycle) Year

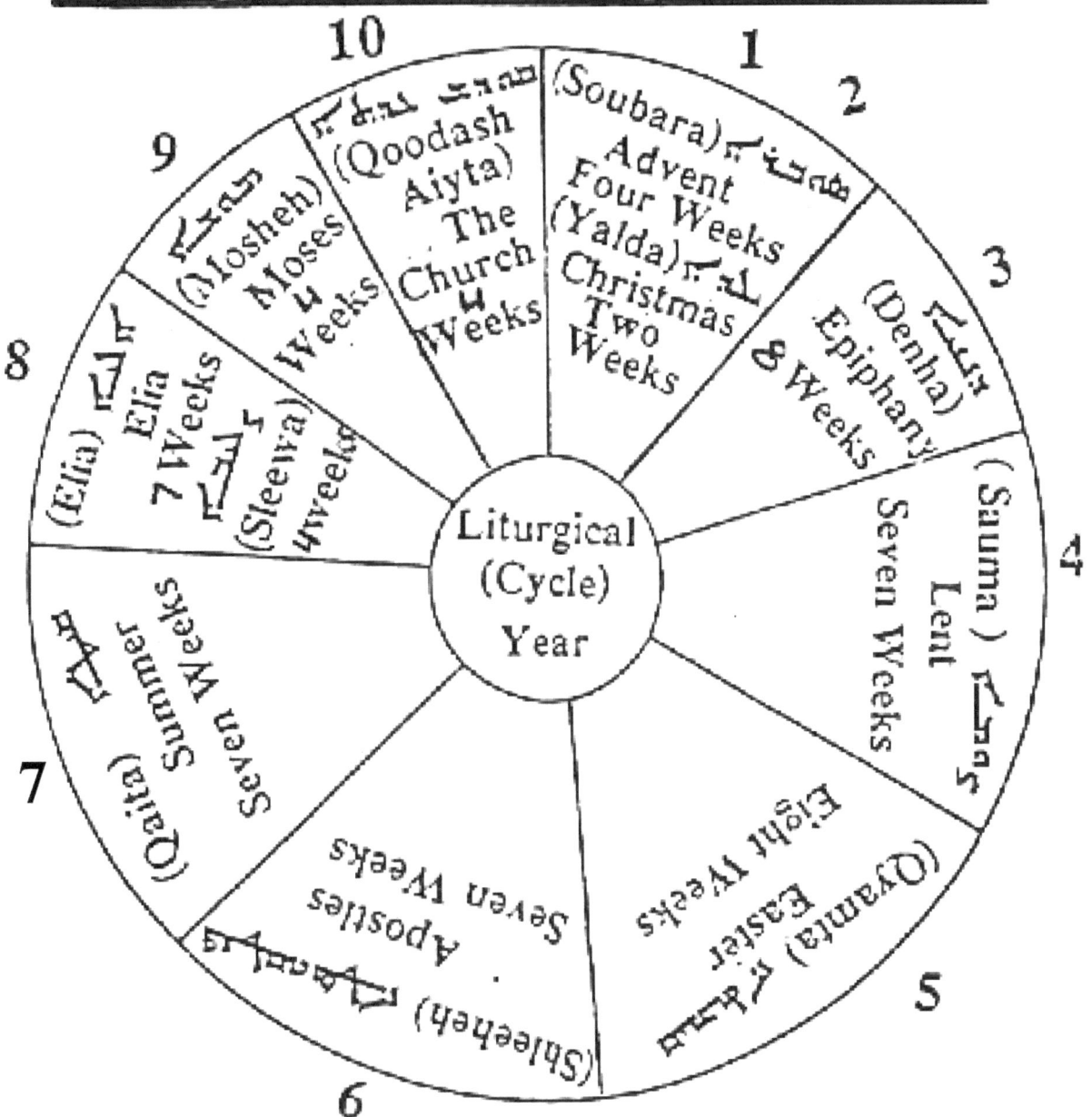

# Chapter IX
# Aramaic – Language of the Chaldeans

The Aramaic language made its historical appearance sometime between 16th – 14th century B.C. in Mesopotamia (in Beth Aramaye, South of Iraq), and Syria, and its alphabet became the vehicle for communication. It became the lingua franca in the ancient near east in the eighth century B.C. and was used from Egypt to Turkey to Pakistan. History recorded that, on 721 B.C., the ten tribes of Israel (the kingdom of the north of Israel) were captured by Assyrians and deported to Nineveh in Mesopotamia. Then the other two tribes, Judah and Benjamin were deported by the Emperor of Chaldeans, Nebuchadnezzar II, in three different exiles 593 B.C., 587 B.C., and 583 B.C., to Babylon in Mesopotamia. The Israelites who returned to Israel in 539 B.C. found their language to be Aramaic; thus, between 721 - 500 B.C., the language of the people of Palestine shifted from Hebrew to Aramaic. Therefore, Jesus and his disciples spoke Aramaic while preaching the message of Christianity in Palestine, Lebanon, Syria, and Mesopotamia. The Aramaic language went through many stages of development:

**1.** Old Aramaic 925-700 B.C.

**2.** Standard Aramaic 700-200 B.C.

**3.** Middle Aramaic 200 B.C.-200 A.D.

**4.** Late Aramaic 200-700 A.D., which includes:

**A. Western Aramaic:** The dialect of the Jews (Jerusalem, the Talmud, and the Targums) and the Syro-Palestine dialect.

**B. Eastern Aramaic:** The dialect of Babylonian-Chaldean form, the Assyrian form, the Syriac form, and the Mundaean form.

The use of the Aramaic language had become common by the period of the Chaldean Empire in Babylon (626-539 B.C.) It became the official language of the imperial government in Mesopotamia and enjoyed general use until the spread of Greek by Alexander the Great (331 B.C.). Yet, even when Greek became the language of choice for literature, culture, politics, and commerce, Aramaic remained the language of the common people until the conquest of the Moslems in the 7th century A.D., which resulted in the spread of Arabic.

The Christians of Iraq, Iran, Syria, Turkey, and Lebanon kept the Aramaic language alive in their homes, schools, and churches. In spite of the pressure of the ruling Arabs to speak Arabic, Modern Aramaic is still spoken today by more than one million people in its many dialects, especially among the Chaldeans, Assyrians, and Syrians. Many Chaldeans emigrated from their country searching for a better life and hoping for a more peaceful and serene atmosphere. They found this atmosphere in the United States because it guarantees life, liberty, and the pursuit of happiness.

Although the Chaldeans are proud of their Middle Eastern culture and heritage, they are also grateful to their new country, America. The Chaldean Liturgy, language and tradition make St. Peter's church a natural center for community gatherings. They meet every Sunday for religious services. They bring their children for Aramaic language classes, for Bible study and for religious instruction. There are many small Chaldean clubs in El Cajon where they meet socially on a regular basis.

Both American-born Chaldeans and those who have emigrated from Mesopotamia have a common challenge to continue to find new avenues through which they can help to keep the Aramaic language and their tradition alive, and to build a better society and become good citizens to the United States of America.

# THE LORD'S PRAYER
ܨܠܘܬܐ ܡܪܢܝܬܐ
## IN ARAMAIC - CHALDEAN

ܐܒܘܢ ܕܒܫܡܝܐ. ܢܬܩܕܫ ܫܡܟ. ܬܐܬܐ
ܡܠܟܘܬܟ. ܢܗܘܐ ܨܒܝܢܟ. ܐܝܟܢܐ ܕܒܫܡܝܐ ܐܦ
ܒܐܪܥܐ.
ܗܒܠܢ ܠܚܡܐ ܕܣܘܢܩܢܢ ܝܘܡܢܐ. ܘܫܒܘܩ ܠܢ
ܚܘܒܝܢ ܘܚܬܗܝܢ. ܐܝܟܢܐ ܕܐܦ ܚܢܢ ܫܒܩܢ
ܠܚܝܒܝܢ. ܘܠܐ ܬܥܠܢ ܠܢܣܝܘܢܐ. ܐܠܐ ܦܨܢ ܡܢ
ܒܝܫܐ. ܡܛܠ ܕܕܝܠܟ ܗܝ ܡܠܟܘܬܐ.
ܘܚܝܠܐ ܘܬܫܒܘܚܬܐ ܠܥܠܡ ܥܠܡܝܢ. ܐܡܝܢ

The Lord's prayer in Aramaic - Chaldean

## 3rd : The Names, Sizes & Styles of the Aramaic alphabet

| # | Arabic | Name | Eng | Aram | Size/Writing | Steps in Aramaic | Name | # |
|---|---|---|---|---|---|---|---|---|
| 1 | أ | Alap | A | | Size 3 over the base line | | | 1 |
| 2 | ب | Beth | B | | Size 2 over the base line | | | 2 |
| 3 | ج | Gamal | G | | Size 3 over the base line & size 1 below line base | | | 3 |
| 4 | د | Dalath | D | | Size 2 over the base line & short horizontal line below | | | 4 |
| 5 | ه | He | H | | Size 2 over the base line | | | 5 |
| 6 | و | Wow | O | | Size 2 over the base line | | | 6 |
| 7 | ز | Zayn | Z | | Size 2 over the base line - size 1 below | | | 7 |
| 8 | ح | Heth | H | | Size 1 over the base line | | | 8 |
| 9 | ط | Teth | T | | Size 3 over the base line - 2 below | | | 9 |
| 10 | ي | Yod | E, I, Y | | Size 1 over the base line | | | 10 |
| 11 | ك | Kap w Kap | C K | | Size 2 over the base line | | | 20 |
| 12 | ل | Lamad | L | | Size 4 over the base line | | | 30 |
| 13 | م | Meem w Meem | M | | size 2 over the base line | | | 40 |
| | | | | | The Final M | | | |
| 14 | ن | Noon w Noon | N | | Size 2 over the base line | | | 50 |
| 15 | س | Simkath | S | | size 2 over the base line | | | 60 |
| 16 | ع | Ae | A | | Size 3 over the base line | | | 70 |
| 17 | ف | Pe | P | | Size 3 over the base line | | | 80 |
| 18 | ص | Sade | S | | Size 1 over the base line - 2 below | | | 90 |
| 19 | ق | Qop | Q | | Size 2 over the base line | | | 100 |
| 20 | ر | Resh | R | | Size 2 over the base line Short horizontal line above | | | 200 |
| 21 | ش | Sheen | Sh | | Size 2 over the base line | | | 300 |
| 22 | ت | Taw w taw | T | | Size 3 over the base line | | | 400 |

# Appendix - A

**Attempted forced change from Chaldean-Aramaic dialect to the Syriac dialect, by the Iraqi government in 1972.**

"In the early 1970s, the Iraqi government tried to suppress Christians in Iraq through passing various laws. On April 16, 1972, the Iraqi government passed an unjust law attempting to change the cultural rights of Christians by changing usage of the Chaldean Aramaic dialect to the Syriac Aramaic dialect. The language of the majority of Christian students, in addition to Arabic, was Chaldean Aramaic. The law mandated that Syriac Aramaic, instead of Chaldean Aramaic, be taught in elementary schools. Syriac Aramaic was also to be taught at intermediate and secondary schools.

In addition, the law formed special programs to be broadcast on public radio and television in Syriac. Three Syriac language magazines were planned to be published in the capital, Baghdad. Also, an association of Syriac speaking authors and writers was established. The bill turned out to be a failure because of non-compliance by the authorities.

The radio stations created as the result of this decree were closed after a few months. While the three Syriac magazines were published, only ten percent of their material was in Syriac."

His Beatitude Paulus Sheikho, the Patriarch of Babylon for the Chaldean Catholic Church, objected to such a law. Sheiko received threats from the Iraqi Government because of his dissent. The majority of Christians in Iraq are Chaldeans and speak the Chaldean Aramaic language.

The late Chaldean Bishop Jacob Manna (1867-1928), author of The Dictionary of Chaldean – Arabic, wrote, "The Greeks invaded Syria and Babylon and called the Aramaic language, 'Syriac' referring to the Syrians." (1900, preface).

Dr. Raphael Bidawid, the Chaldean Patriarch of Babylon, reprinted Manna's dictionary in 1975. In Bidawid's introduction, he wrote that historically Syrians were called Arameans. Bidawid also wrote that the name of their language, Syriac, came to Iraqi Christians after receiving Jesus' disciples from Israel and Syria to Iraq."

The truth is, our language is the Chaldean Aramaic dialect.

Original in Arabic, by Sam Gammo, Sydney, Australia, Feb. 19, 2016.

# Appendix - B

## Chaldeans in the Bible

| | Chaldea (14) | | 24:5 | Chaldees | | 27:20 | | 3:95 |
|---|---|---|---|---|---|---|---|---|
| Jdt | 2:23 | | 25:12 | Neh | 9:7 | 3:98 | | 3:98 |
| Is | 48:14 | | 32:4 | Nebuchadnezzar (111) | | 28:11 | | 4:1 |
| | 48:20 | | 32:5 | 2 Kgs | 24:1 | 4:15 | | 4:15 |
| Jer | 50:10 | | 32:24 | | 24:10 | 4:25 | | 4:25 |
| | 51:1 | | 32:25 | | 24:11 | 4:28 | | 4:28 |
| | 51:4 | | 32:28 | | 25:1 | 4:30 | | 4:30 |
| | 51:24 | | 32:29 | | 25:8 | 4:31 | | 4:31 |
| | 51:35 | | 32:43 | | 25:22 | 4:34 | | 4:34 |
| Ez | 11:24 | | 33:5 | 1 Chr | 5:41 | 5:2 | | 5:2 |
| | 16:29 | | 35:11 | 2 Chr | 36:6 | 5:11 | | 5:11 |
| | 23:15 | | 37:5 | | 36:7 | 39:5 | | 5:18 |
| | 23:16 | | 37:8 | | 36:10 | 39:11 | | Nebuchadnezzar's |
| | 23:23 | | 37:9 | | 36:13 | 43:10 | Dn | 3:19 |
| H b | 1:6 | | 37:13 | Ezr | 1:7 | 44:30 | | |
| | Chaldean (13) | | 37:14 | | 2:1 | 46:2 | Ur of Chaldeans (4) | |
| 2 Kgs | 25:5 | | 38:12 | | 5:12 | 46:13 | Gn | 11:28 |
| | 25:10 | | 38:18 | | 5:14 | 46:26 | | 11:31 |
| | 25:24 | | 38:19 | | 6:5 | 49:28 | | 15:7 |
| Ezr | 5:12 | | 38:23 | Neh | 7:6 | 49:30 | Neh | 9:7 |
| Jer | 37:10 | | 39:8 | Jdt | 1:1 | 50:17 | | |
| | 37:11 | | 40:9 | | 1:5 | 51:34 | | |
| | 39:5 | | 40:10 | | 1:7 | 52:4 | | |
| | 41:3 | | 41:18 | | 1:11 | 52:12 | | |
| | 51:5 | | 43:3 | | 1:12 | 52:28 | | |
| | 52:8 | | 50:1 | | 2:1 | 52:29 | | |
| | 52:14 | | 50:8 | | 2:4 | 52:30 | | |
| Dn | 2:10 | | 50:25 | | 2:19 | Bar | 1:9 | |
| | 5:30 | | 50:35 | | 3:2 | | 1:11 | |
| | Chaldeans (70) | | 50:45 | | 3:8 | | 1:12 | |
| Gn | 11:28 | | 51:54 | | 4:1 | | 6:1 | |
| | 11:31 | | 52:7 | | 6:2 | Ez | 26:7 | |
| | 15:7 | | 52:17 | | 6:3 | | 29:18 | |
| 2 Kgs | 24:2 | Bar | 1:2 | | 6:4 | | 29:19 | |
| | 25:4 | | 6:40 | | 11:1 | | 30:10 | |
| | 25:13 | Ez | 1:3 | | 11:4 | Dn | 1:1 | |
| | 25:25 | | 12:13 | | 11:7 | | 1:18 | |
| | 25:26 | | 23:14 | | 11:23 | | 2:1 | |
| 2 Chr | 36:17 | Dn | 1:4 | | 12:13 | | 2:28 | |
| Jdt | 5:6 | | 2:2 | | 14:18 | | 2:46 | |
| | 5:7 | | 2:4 | Est | A:3 | | 3:1 | |
| Jb | 1:17 | | 2:5 | | 2:6 | | 3:3 | |
| Is | 13:19 | | 2:10 | Jer | 21:2 | | 3:5 | |
| | 23:13 | | 3:8 | | 21:7 | | 3:7 | |
| | 43:14 | | 3:48 | | 22:25 | | 3:9 | |
| | 47:1 | | 4:4 | | 24:1 | | 3:13 | |
| | 47:5 | | 5:7 | | 25:1 | | 3:14 | |
| Jer | 21:4 | | 5:11 | | 25:9 | | 3:16 | |
| | 21:9 | | 9:1 | | 27:6 | | 3:91 | |
| | 22:25 | ACTS | 7:4 | | 27:8 | | 3:93 | |

# BIBLIOGRAPHY

Bazzi M. J., *Tilkepe: Present and Past* (in Arabic). Fr. Bazzi, 1969.

Beek M. A., *Atlas of Mesopotamia.* Thomas Nelson and Sons Ltd., 1962.

*The New Encyclopedia Britannica.* Vol. II, William Penton, Publisher, 1974.

Fitzmyre J. A., *A Wandering Aramean.* Scholars Press, 1979.

Guliana S., *History of Mesopotamia* (in Aramaic), Guliana, 1979.

Lloyd S., *The Archeology of Mesopotamia.* Thomas and Hadson Ltd., 1978.

McGovern et al. (1992, Nov.). *Chemical Evidence for Ancient Beer. Nature.* 360(6399) 24.

Oppenheim L. A., *Ancient Mesopotamia.* The University of Chicago Press, 1977.

Parrot A., *Babylonia E L'Antico Testamento.* Edlizione Paoline, 1973.

Parrot A., *Nineva E L'Antico Testamento.* Edlizione Paoline, 1972.

Pew Research Center. (2017). April 5, 2017. *The Global Religious Landscape. [Report]. https://www.pewforum.org/2017/04/05/the-changing-global-religious-landscape/*

Prichard J. B., *Ancient Near East in Pictures.* 2nd ed. Princeton University Press, 1969.

Prichard J. B., *Ancient Near Eastern Texts.* 2nd ed., Princeton University Press, 1955.

Roux G., *Ancient Iraq.* 2nd ed., The Chancer Press, 1982.

Thompson J. A., *The Bible and Archaeology.* Wm. B. Eerdmans Publishing Co., 1960.

United States Conference of Catholic Bishops. 2nd. Ed. *New American Bible.* Saint Benedict Press, 2001.

Young G., *Iraq Land of Two Rivers.* William Collins and Co. Ltd, 1980.

**Other Titles by Let in the Light Publishing:**
*Aramaic Language Chaldean Dialogue*
*Beginner's Handbook of the Aramaic Chaldean Alphabets*
*Chaldeans Present and Past*
*Classical Aramaic I*
*Classical Aramaic II*
*A High School Tennis Coach's Handbook: For Players, Parents, and Coaches*
*Preserving the Chaldean Aramaic Language*
*Read and Write the Modern Aramaic*
*The Advanced Handbook of Modern Aramaic Dialect*
*The Life of Tilkepnaye*
*Tilkepe: Past and Present*
*Who are the Chaldeans?*
*Know your Faith*


To order, please visit: www.letinthelightpublishing.com.
Let in the Light looks forward to serving you!

# About the Author

Fr. Michael J. Bazzi (Emeritus) was born in Tilkepe, Iraq in 1938 to Catholic parents. In 1954, he entered St. Peter's Catholic Seminary in Mosul, Iraq. After 10 years he was ordained a priest in Baghdad on May 15, 1964. He served in Tilkepe from 1964-1972. As assistant priest, he worked with youth, establishing Bible study groups. Bazzi published Tilkepe: Present and Past in Arabic in 1969. From 1972-1974 he studied Pastoral Theology in Rome at the Lateran University. Bazzi received a Master's degree in Pastoral Theology as well as diplomas in Mass Media and Group Dynamics.

Arriving in the United States on June 20, 1974, Bazzi taught scripture for five years in Oshkosh, Wisconsin (Greenbay Diocese) and four years in Michigan, where he established two churches. In 1983, he moved to Los Angeles where he served as a pastor of St. Paul's parish in Montrose and on September 1, 1985, Bazzi moved to San Diego and became assistant pastor at St. Peter's Parish. In 1987, Fr. Bazzi became pastor of St. Peter's Parish. He worked with adults and youth, establishing Bible Study groups and teaching Catechism and Aramaic language in its Chaldean dialect. In 1989, he established St. Michael's Chaldean Catholic parish in El Cajon. At St. Peter's Parish he established three projects for the community:
1) St. Peter's Church Hall 2) Education Center 3) The large rectory.

Professor Bazzi has been teaching the Chaldean Dialect of the Aramaic Language at Cuyamaca College since 1989. Bazzi has published several textbooks on modern and classical Aramaic including: *Classical Aramaic I & II, Modern Aramaic Vol. I & II, Beginners Handbook of the Aramaic Language*, a children's book called *Read and Write Aramaic, the Divine Liturgy, The Life of Tilkepnaye*

| Photo No. | Caption | الشرح | رقم الصورة |
|---|---|---|---|
| (1) | Hammurabi receiving the laws from God Mardokh | حمورابي يستلم القوانين من إله مردوخ | (١) |
| (2) | The Babylonian Merchants | تُجار بابل | (٢) |
| (3) | World map according in the time of Babylon | خارطة العالم في العهد البابلي | (٣) |
| (4) | Winged Bull with Human Head | الثور المجنح برأس انسان | (٤) |
| (5) | Gate of Ishtar in Babylon | بوابة عشتار في بابل | (٥) |
| (6) | Hanging Gardens of Babylon | الجنائن المعلقة في بابل | (٦) |
| (7) | City of Babylon | مدينة بابل | (٧) |
| (8) | Entrance to Babylon | المدخل الى مدينة بابل | (٨) |
| (9) | Hammurabi | حورابي | (٩) |
| (10) | Chaldean dynasty 625-539 B.C. | السلالات البابلية ٦٢٥-٥٣٩ ق.م | (١٠) |
| (11) | Side of Ishtar gate | جانب من بوابة عشتار | (١١) |
| (12) | Babylon is famous with palms trees | اشتهرت بابل بأشجار النخيل | (١٢) |
| (13) (14) (15) | Mythical animals erected on the walls of Babylon | رموز الحيوانات الاسطورية المحفورة على الجدران في مدينة بابل | (١٣) (١٤) (١٥) |
| (16) | Lion of Babylon Keeper of the Defenseless | أسد بابل حامي الضعفاء | (١٦) |
| (17) | Lion of Babylon on the wall | أسد بابل محفور على الجدار | (١٧) |

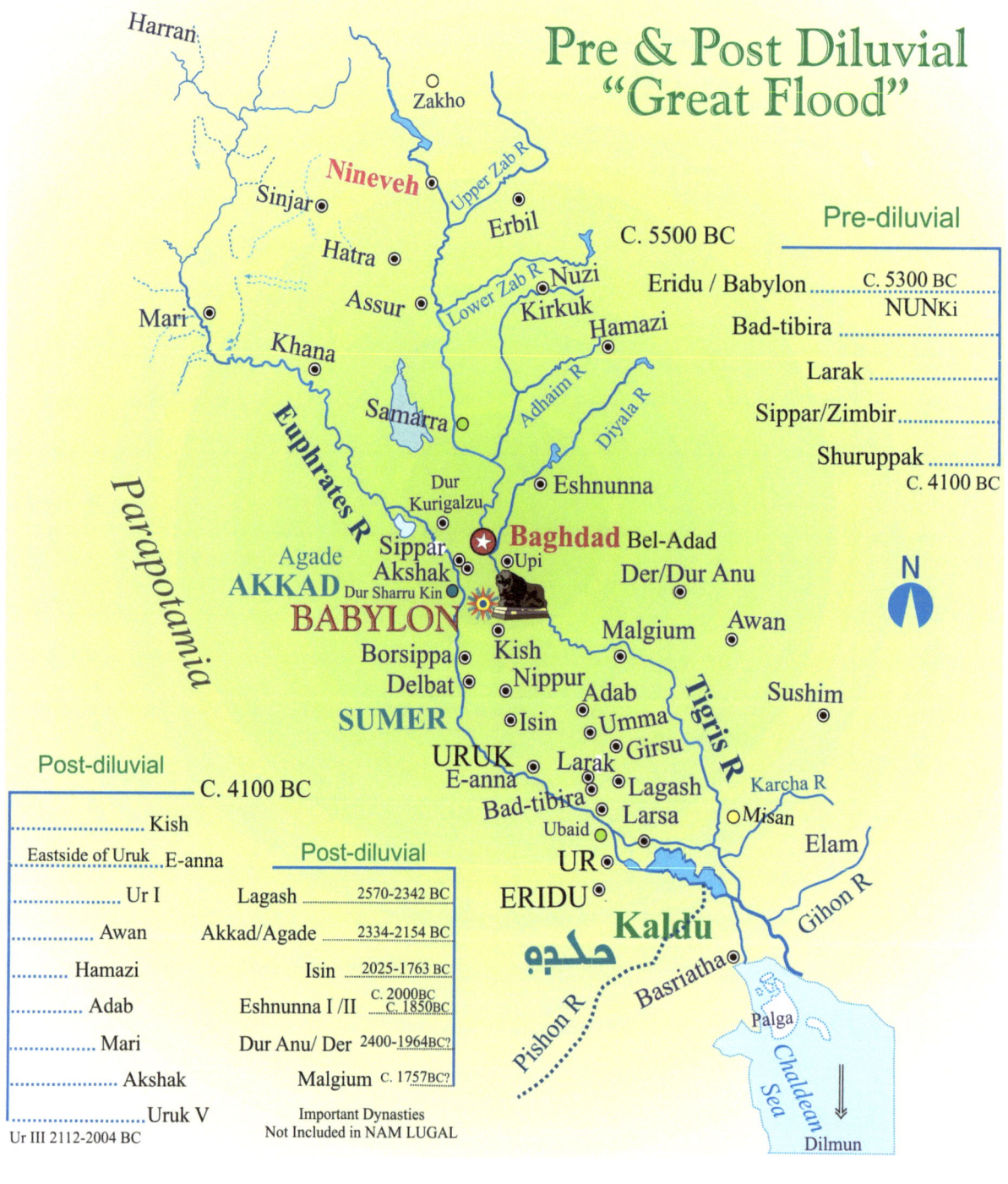

# Ancient MESOPOTAMIA

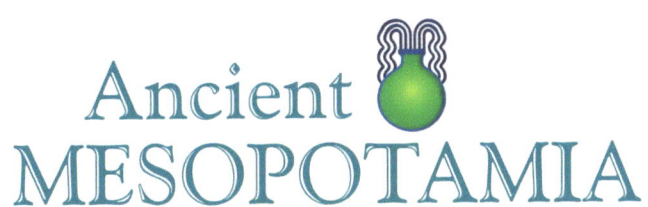

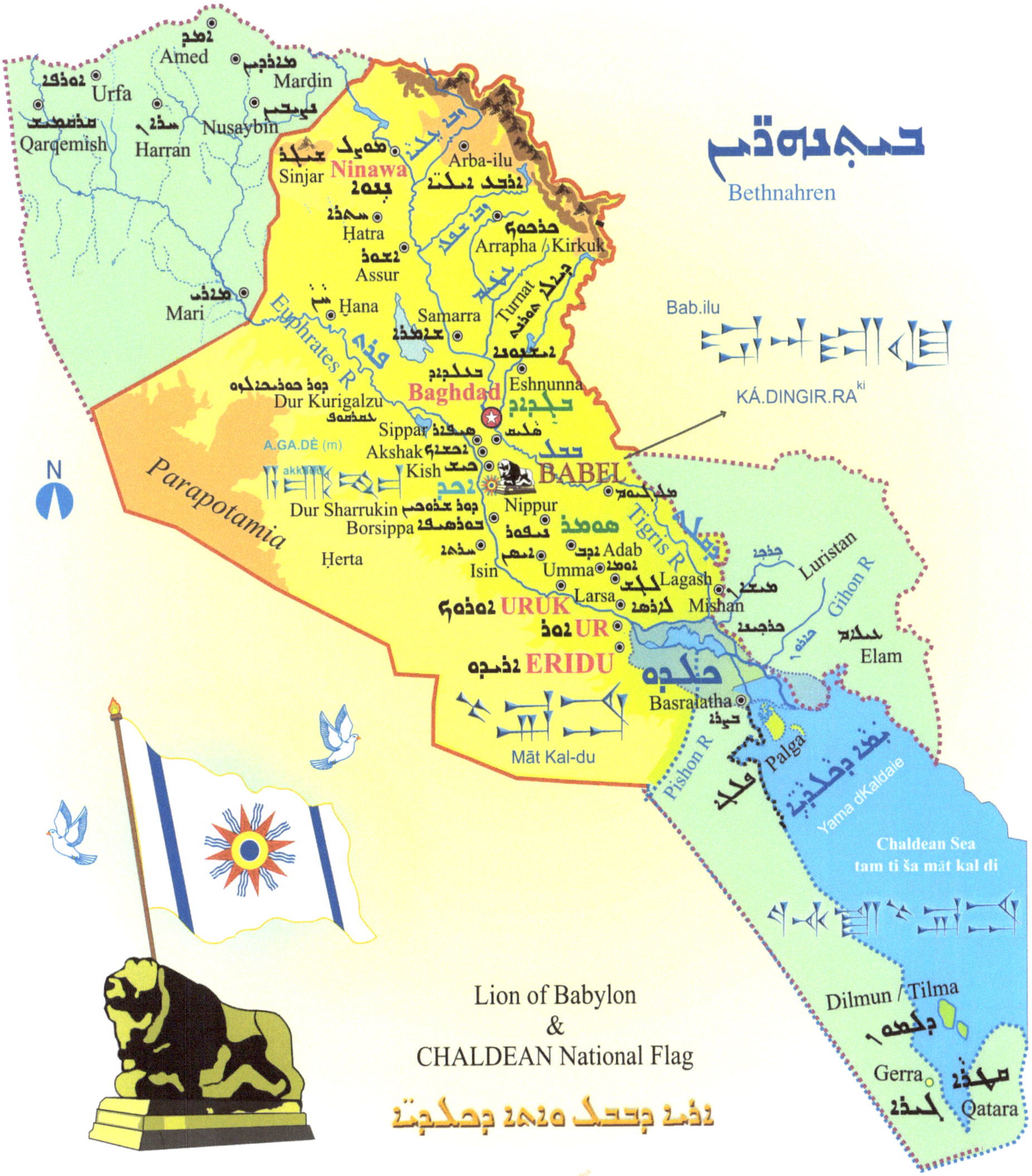


Lion of Babylon
&
CHALDEAN National Flag

أسد بابل حامي الضعفاء
Lion of Babylon Keeper of the Defenseless
صورة رقم (١٦)   Photo No. (16)

أسد بابل محفور على الجدار
Lion of Babylon on the wall
صورة رقم (١٧)   Photo No. (17)

رموز الحيوانات الاسطورية المحفورة على الجدران في مدينة بابل
Mythical animals erected on the walls of Babylon

صورة رقم (١٣)    Photo No. (13)

صورة رقم (١٤)    Photo No. (14)

صورة رقم (١٥)    Photo No. (15)

حمورابي
Hammurabi
Photo No. (9) صورة رقم (٩)

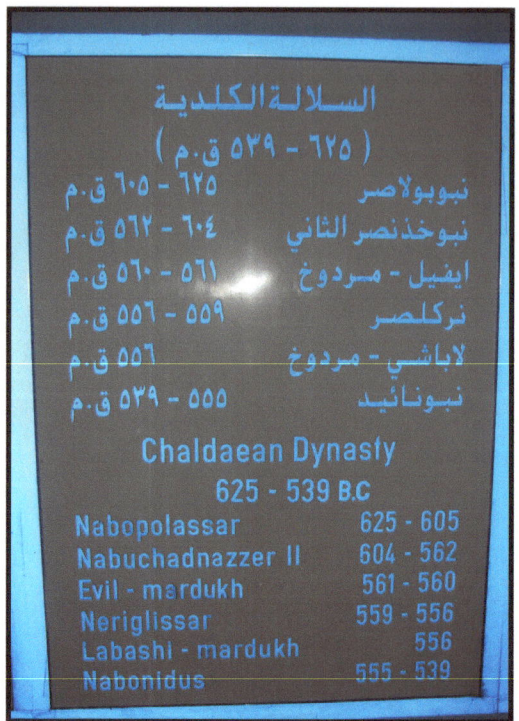

السلالات البابلية ٦٢٥-٥٣٩ ق.م
Chaldean dynasty 625-539 B.C.
Photo No. (10) صورة رقم (١٠)

جانب من بوابة عشتار
Side of Ishtar gate
Photo No. (11) صورة رقم (١١)

اشتهرت بابل بأشجار النخيل
Babylon is famous with palms trees
Photo No. (12) صورة رقم (١٢)

مدينة بابل
City of Babylon
صورة رقم (٧)     Photo No. (7)

المدخل الى مدينة بابل
Entrance to Babylon
صورة رقم (٨)     Photo No. (8)

بوابة عشتار في بابل
Gate of Ishtar in Babylon
صورة رقم (٥)     Photo No. (5)

الجنائن المعلقة في بابل
Hanging Gardens of Babylon
صورة رقم (٦)     Photo No. (6)

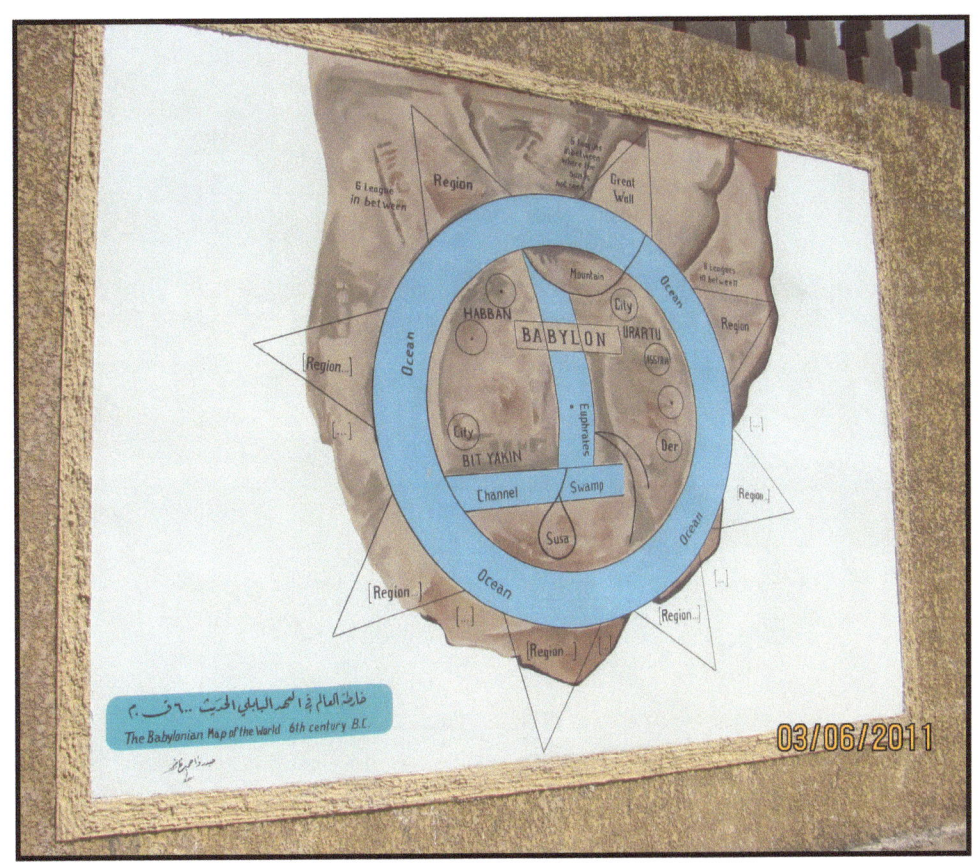

خارطة العالم في العهد البابلي
World map according in the time of Babylon
صورة رقم (٣) Photo No. (3)

الثور المجنح برأس انسان
Winged Bull with Human Head
صورة رقم (٤) Photo No. (4)

حمورابي يستلم القوانين من إله مردوخ
Hammurabi receiving the laws from God Mardokh

صورة رقم (١)     Photo No. (1)

تُجار بابل
The Babylonian Merchants

صورة رقم (٢)     Photo No. (2)

# الملحـــق

الإعتراف والتغيير الإجباري للغة الكلدانية إلى السريانية مِن قِبَل الحكومة العراقية في عام ١٩٧٢. بقلم سام گمو

في مطلع السبعينات حاولت الحكومة العراقية قمع المسيحيين في العراق من خلال إصدار مختلف القوانين. في ٢٠ فبراير ١٩٧٢ أصدرت الحكومة قانون منح الحقوق الثقافية للناطقين بالسريانية عن طريق تغيير اللغة الكلدانية إلى السريانية، والسماح بتدريس السريانية في المدارس ذات الغالبية من الطلاب المتحدثين بتلك اللغة بالإضافة إلى اللغة العربية ولكن لم تطبّق. وان غبطة بولس شيخو بطريرك بابل للكنيسة الكلدانية الكاثوليكية اعترض على هذا القانون. لكنه تلقّى تهديدا من الحكومة العراقية، وغالبية المسيحيّين في العراق هم كلدانيّون يتكلمون اللغة الكلدانية. وكان من المقرر نشر ثلاث مجلات باللغة السريانية في العاصمة، وأنشأوا جمعية الناطقين والكتّاب والمؤلفين بالسريانية، وأنْ تذاع برامج خاصة في الإذاعة والتلفزيون العام.

إن مشروع القانون فشل، وبعد بضعة أشهر أُغلقت المحطات الإذاعية التي تم إنشاؤها نتيجة لهذا المرسوم، في حين سمح بنشر مجلتين فقط و ١٠ % من موادها كانت باللغة السريانية، ولم يُسمح للمدارس أن تسمى هذه اللغة بالكلدانية.

نشر المطران الكلداني أوجين منّا (١٨٦٧-١٩٧٥) القاموس الكلداني العربي (عام ١٩٠٠) وأعاد طبعه في عام ١٩٧٥ الدكتور روفائيل بيداويذ بطريرك بابل على الكلدان، وجاء في مقدمته صفحة ص١٧ اليونانيون غزوا سوريا وبابل فسمّوا اللغة الكلدانية بالسريانية نسبة إلى الشعب السوري.

وبصورة عامة السوريون لم يسموا بهذا الإسم أبداً، بل كانوا يسمون آراميون، إسم السريانية جاءنا من خلال تلاميذ المسيح من إسرائيل وسوريا، والحقيقة لغتنا هي اللغة الكلدانية.

نادي بابل/ بقلم سام گمو

ما بين النهرين وتمتعت باستخدامها بشكل عام حتى انتشار اليونانية من قبل الإسكندر الأكبر (٣٣١ قبل الميلاد). ومع ذلك، حتى عندما أصبحت اليونانية اللغة المفضلة للأدب والثقافة والسياسة والتجارة، ظلت الآرامية لغة عامة الناس حتى غزوات المسلمين في القرن السابع الميلادي، مما أدى إلى انتشار اللغة العربية.

حافظ مسيحيو العراق وإيران وسوريا وتركيا ولبنان على اللغة الآرامية حية في منازلهم ومدارسهم وكنائسهم. على الرغم من الضغوط التي مارسها الحكام العرب على المسيحيين للتكلم باللغة العربية، لا تزال الآرامية الحديثة يتحدث بها اليوم أكثر من مليون شخص بلهجاتها العديدة، وخاصة بين الكلدان (اللهجة الآرامية الكلدانية)، والآشوريين (اللهجة الآرامية - الآشورية)، والسريان. (اللهجة الآرامية السريانية).

هاجر العديد من الكلدان من بلادهم بحثاً عن حياة أفضل وجو أكثر هدوءاً. لقد وجدوا هذا الجو في بعض البلدان الأوربية وأستراليا وبالأخص في الولايات المتحدة التي تتوفر فيها الحياة الكريمة والحرية والسعادة والعيش الرغيد. على الرغم من أن الكلدان في الولايات المتحدة فخورون بثقافتهم وتراثهم الشرق أوسطي، إلا أنهم يدينون بالولاء لموطنهم الجديد أمريكا.

إن اليتورجية الكلدانية تجعل القداس الكلداني واللغة والتقاليد في كاتدرائية القديس بطرس مركزاً طبيعياً للتجمعات. يجتمعون كل يوم أحد للمشاركة في الاحتفال بالقداس الإلهي؛ ويجلبون أطفالهم على مدار الأسبوع للنشاطات الدينية والاجتماعية المختلفة، ويجتمع الشباب والكبار لدرس الآرامية - الكلدانية والكتاب المقدس جنباً إلى جنب مع دروس التعليم المسيحي؛ على مدار الأسبوع.

يواجه كل من الكلدان المولودين في الولايات المتحدة وأولئك الذين هاجروا من بلاد ما بين النهرين تحدياً مشتركاً لمواصلة البحث عن طرق جديدة تمكنهم من خلالها الاستمرار في الحفاظ على اللغة الآرامية - الكلدانية والتقاليد المسيحية التي تربّوا عليها، وبناء مجتمع أفضل، وأن يصبحوا مواطنين صالحين للولايات المتحدة الأمريكية وطنهم الجديد.

أقدّم شكري وامتناني لسيادة المطران مار سرهد يوسب جمّو الجزيل الاحترام، لمراجعته هذا الكتاب ومشاركته بملاحظات مفيدة وقيّمة.
وهو الخبير بتاريخ الأمة الكلدانية وحاضرها.

# الفصل التاسع
# اللغة الآرامية لغة الكلدان

ظهرت اللغة الآرامية في تاريخها بين القرنين السادس والرابع عشر قبل الميلاد. في بلاد ما بين النهرين (في بيث أرامايي، جنوب العراق)، وسوريا، وأصبحت أبجديتها وسيلة للتواصل. أصبحت لغة مشتركة في الشرق الأدنى القديم في القرن الثامن قبل الميلاد. وتمّ استخدامها في مصر وتركيا وباكستان. سجّل التاريخ أنه في عام ٧٢١ قبل الميلاد، تمّ الاستيلاء على أسباط إسرائيل العشرة (مملكة شمال إسرائيل) من قبل الآشوريين وترحيلهم إلى نينوى في بلاد ما بين النهرين. ثم تمّ ترحيل السبطَين الآخرين، يهوذا وبنيامين، من قبل إمبراطور الكلدانيين، نبوخذ نصر الثاني، في ثلاثة ازمان مختلفة ٥٩٣ قبل الميلاد و٥٨٧ قبل الميلاد و٥٨٣ قبل الميلاد الى بابل في بلاد ما بين النهرين. لذلك فان بني إسرائيل الذين عادوا إلى إسرائيل عام ٥٣٩ قبل الميلاد. أصبحت لغتهم الآرامية. وهكذا، بين ٧٢١ - ٥٠٠ قبل الميلاد، انتقلت لغة شعب فلسطين من العبرية إلى الآرامية. لذلك، تحدث يسوع وتلاميذه باللغة الآرامية أثناء التبشير برسالة المسيحية في فلسطين ولبنان وسوريا وبلاد ما بين النهرين. مرت اللغة الآرامية بمراحل عديدة من التطور:

١- الآرامية القديمة ٩٢٥-٧٠٠ قبل الميلاد

٢- الآرامية القياسية ٧٠٠-٢٠٠ قبل الميلاد

٣- الآرامية الوسطى ٢٠٠ ق.م - ٢٠٠ م

٤- الآرامية المتأخرة ٢٠٠-٧٠٠ م وتشمل

أ. الآرامية الغربية: لهجة اليهود (اورشليم والتلمود والتارغوم) واللهجة السورية الفلسطينية.

ب. الآرامية الشرقية: بـ ٤ لهجات ١- البابلية الكلدانية ٢- اللهجة الآشورية ٣- اللهجة السريانية و٤- الصيغة المندائية.

أصبح استخدام اللغة الآرامية شائعًا في فترة الإمبراطورية الكلدانية في بابل (٦٢٦-٥٣٩ قبل الميلاد) وأصبحت اللغة الرسمية للحكومة الإمبراطورية في بلاد

# The Chaldean Liturgical (Cycle) Year

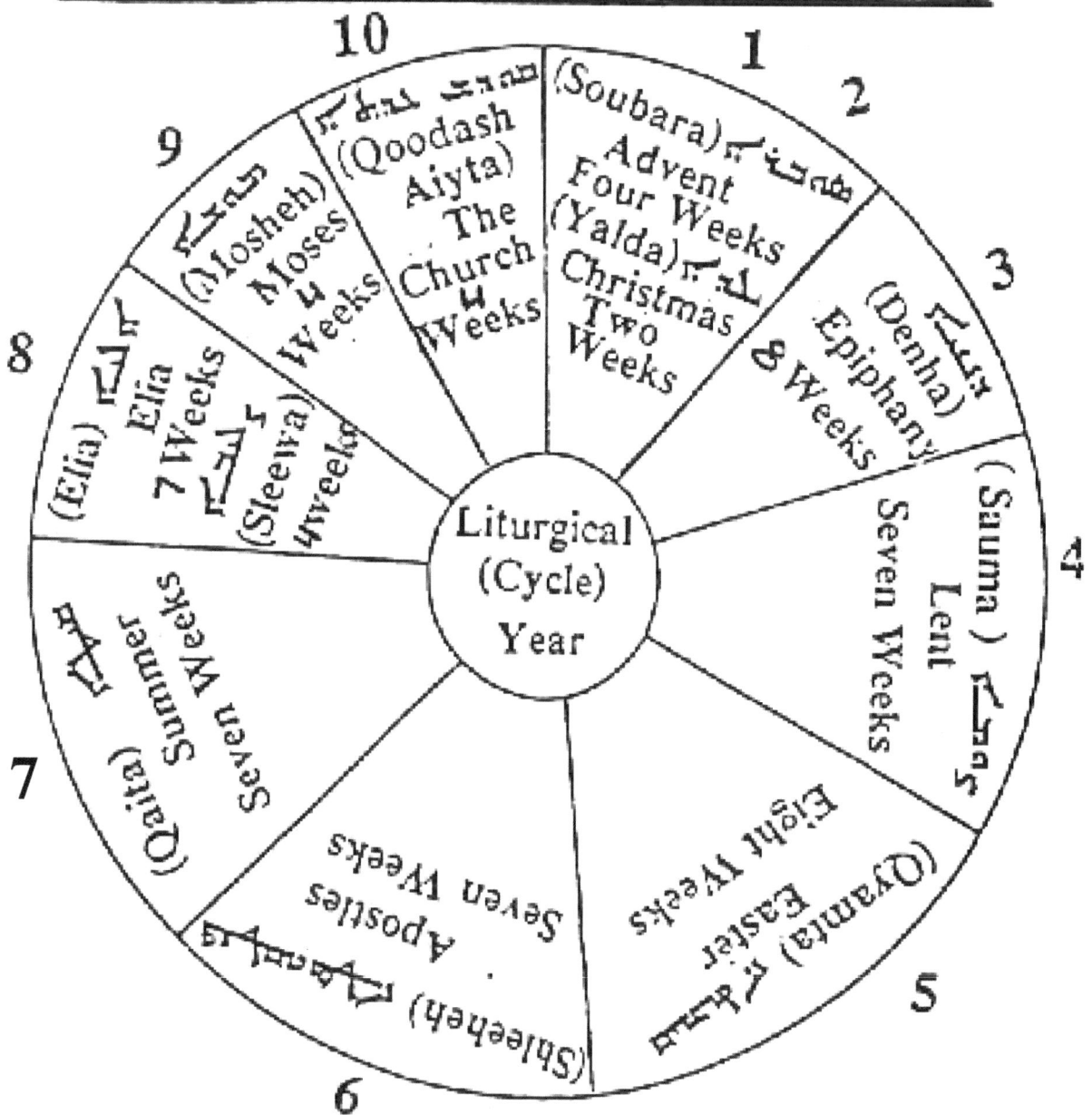

# الفصـل الثامـن
# الطقـس الكلدانـي

يتمّ استخدام الطقس الكلداني من قبل الناس الذين موطنهم بلاد ما بين النهرين وبابل وآشور. بعد ان تلقّوا رسالة الإنجيل من القديس توما الرسول، ومار أدّاي، واثنين من تلاميذ أدي القديسين ماري وأجّاي. يعود الفضل إلى أداي وماري في إنشاء صيغة التقديس الليتورجية الأولى.

### السنة الليتورجية حسب الطقوس الكلدانية الشرقية

تمّ ترتيب الدورة الليتورجية التي يستخدمها الكلدان اليوم في القرن السابع الميلادي خلال بطريركية ايشوعياب حذيّاوايا. تعكس الدورة خطة الله لخلاص البشرية، من البشارة (ولادة المسيح) وحتى باروسيا (المجيء الثاني للمسيح.) وهي مقسمة إلى عدة مواسم تدعى الشاووعه.

معظم الشاووعه تتكون من سبعة أسابيع، بينما يختلف البعض الآخر من سنة إلى أخرى. يتكون أول وآخر الشاووعه دائماً من أربعة أسابيع. في بعض منها العدد ثابت لا يتغير.

القداس الكلداني قديم جداً ينسب الى الرسولين أداي وماري. تستخدم اللغة الآرامية كلغة رئيسية.

٤- **الكنائس المستقلة الأخرى**: تتمتع هذه الكنائس بأدنى درجة من الاستقلالية الكنسية، وهي بالكاد أعلى من أي أبرشية / أبرشية أخرى.

الكنائس ذات التسلسل الهرمي هي: ١٣. الكنيسة البلغارية ١٤. الكنيسة اليونانية ١٥. الكنيسة الهنغارية ١٦. الكنيسة الإيطالية الألبانية ١٧. الكنيسة السلوفاكية ١٨. الكنيسة اليوغوسلافية والكنائس بدون تسلسل هرمي هي: ١٩. الكنيسة البيلاروسية ٢٠. الكنيسة الألبانية ٢١. الكنيسة الجورجية ٢٢. الكنيسة الروسية.

كانت الكنائس الشرقية ضمن الإمبراطورية الرومانية الرئيسية هي روما واورشليم لاحقا وأنطاكية، والإسكندرية، والبيزنطية، الملابارية، الارمنية والكلدانية خارج الإمبراطورية الرومانية.

تنقسم كل من الكنائس الشرقية إلى أقسام فرعية، تستخدم في الغالب لغتها الخاصة ولها تعديلاتها الخاصة في القانون والليتورجيا. يستخدم طقس أنطاكية الآرامية كلغة رئيسية. تستمد اسمها من مدينة أنطاكية في سوريا، حيث تم تسمية أتباع المسيح لأول مرة مسيحيين حوالي عام ٤٠م (أعمال الرسل ١١: ٢٦).

الكنائس الشرقية تشمل الكنيسة الكلدانية الآشورية، التي تستخدم اللغة الآرامية، والكنيسة المالابارية. تحتوي الكنائس الغربية الأنطاكية على الكنائس السورية والمالنكارية والمارونية. الكنيسة القبطية تستخدم اللغة القبطية كلغة رئيسية للاحتفال بطقوسها وتستخدمها الكنائس القبطية والإثيوبية. تستخدم الكنيسة البيزنطية اليونانية كلغة رئيسية لها اليوم، تُنظم الحياة الكنسية للكنائس الشرقية الكاثوليكية وفقًا لقانون شرائع الكنائس الشرقية (CCEO) الذي أصدره البابا يوحنا بولس الثاني في ١٨ أكتوبر ١٩٩٠ وبدأ القانون في ١ أكتوبر، ١٩٩١. وفقا للقانون الشرقي الجديد، تنقسم الكنائس الشرقية الكاثوليكية إلى أربع فئات:

١- **البطريركية**: يرأسها بطريرك له سلطة على المطارنة والأساقفة وغيرهم من المؤمنين المسيحيين في كنيسته وفقاً لشكل القانون. الكنائس البطريركية هي: ١. الكنيسة الكلدانية ٢. الكنيسة الأرمنية ٣. الكنيسة القبطية ٤. الكنيسة السريانية ٥. الكنيسة المارونية ٦. الكنيسة الملكية. ٧. الكنيسة الأوكرانية

٢- **رئاسات الأساقفة**: يحكمها رئيس أساقفة رئيسي. إن قوته وسلطات سينودس الأساقفة مساوية لسلطات البطريرك وسينودس الأساقفة للكنيسة البطريركية. تضم:
٨- كنيسة مالابار

٣- **متروبوليتان مستقل**: يترأسه متروبوليتان، والذي يجب تمييزه عن العاصمة التي تترأس مقاطعة كنسية تابعة للكنيسة البطريركية التابعة للكنيسة Archiepiscopal. وتشمل هذه: ٩. الكنيسة الإثيوبية ١٠. كنيسة سيرو مالانكارا ١١. الكنيسة الأمريكية الروثينية ١٢. الكنيسة الرومانية.

# الفصل السابع
## الكنائس الشرقية الكاثوليكية

انتشرت المسيحية في القرون الأولى بسرعة في جميع أنحاء الشرق الأوسط القديم وأوروبا والبلدان التي كانت تقع شرق البحر الأبيض المتوسط، كان لها طقوس خاصة بها، والتي يتم الاحتفال بها بلغاتهم المحلية. وقد أطلق آباء الكنيسة على هذه الليتورجيات الطقوس الشرقية. بينما احتفلت روما، الواقعة غرب البحر الأبيض المتوسط، بالطقوس الدينية حسب الطقس الروماني الغربي (اللاتيني).

إن الكنيسة الكاثوليكية هي مشاركة مع كنائس خاصة في الشرق والغرب. تُعرف هذه باسم «الكنائس الطقسية ذات الطابع الخاص» (باللاتينية «لقانونها الخاص» أو «المستقلة»)، والتي تشير إلى وضعها القانوني على أنها تتمتع بالقدرة على حكم نفسها وفقًا لقوانينها الخاصة. كل من الكنائس الشرقية الكاثوليكية هي كنيسة مستقلة.

تضمّ الكنيسة الكاثوليكية حاليًا ثلاث وعشرين كنيسة مستقلة تتمتع بالحكم الذاتي في الأساس تحت حكم الحبر الروماني، الذي هم معه في شركة كاملة وتتحقق فيها الشركة الشاملة.

فيما يلي قائمة بالكنائس الكاثوليكية المستقلة مرتبة حسب التقاليد التي تتبعها:

أولاً: الإسكندري: ١- القبطية ٢- الإثيوبية

ثانياً: الانطاكي: ٣- مالنكار ٤- ماروني ٥- سوري

ثالثاً: القسطنطيني: ٦- الألباني ٧- البيلاروسي ٨- البلغاري ٩- اليوناني ١٠- الهنغاري ١١- الإيطالي – الألباني ١٢- الملكي ١٣- الروماني ١٤- الروسي ١٥- الروثياني ١٦- السلوفاكي ١٧- الأوكراني ١٨- يوغسلافي ١٩- الجورجي

رابعاً: الأرمني: ٢٠- أرمني

خامساً: الكلداني: ٢١- كلداني ٢٢- مالابار

سادساً: لاتيني (غربي): ٢٣- روماني

٢٩ آب ٢٠١٧: تراس البطريرك لويس ساكو حفلة تنصيب المطران عمانويل حنا شليطا مطرانا على كاتدرائية القديس بطرس في كاتدرائية القديس بطرس الكلدانية الكاثوليكية.

ولد المطران عمانوئيل شليطا ١١ ت٢ ١٩٥٦ في فيشخابور – زاخو. رُسم كاهنا في روما ١٩٨٤ وحصل على شهادة الدكتوراء في اللاهوت الكتابي. جاء الى الولايات المتحدة ١٩٨٧ وعمل في خورنة مار بولس في لوس انجلوس وعام ٢٠٠٠ انتقل الى ديترويت. عمل في خورنة مار يوسف، ثم في خورنة مار كيوركيس. ٢٠١٥ نال الدرجة الأسقفية وتعين مطرانا في كندا، وعام ٢٠١٧ تعين في سانديكو.

٣١ ت٢ عام ٢٠١٧ البابا فرنسيس عيّن مار باواي سورو اسقفا لمطرانية مار أدّي للكلدان في تورونتو – كندا.

المدعي العام (١٩٩٣-١٩٩٨) يلاحق جناية وجرائم جنحة ارتكبت من ناشيونال سيتي جنوب الحدود المكسيكية، والجرائم والجنح التي ارتكبها الأحداث في مقاطعة سانديكو، وأعضاء عصابات الشوارع بسبب العنف جرائم جنائية. تخرج من جامعة كاليفورنيا، سانتا باربرا (بكالوريوس، تاريخ/علوم سياسية، ١٩٧٨)، وكلية الحقوق بجامعة سانديكو (١٩٨٢). الوظيفة الحالية للحاكم بيتر دڈه ستنتهي في ٦ يناير ٢٠٢٥.

**١١ كانون الثاني ٢٠١٤**: عيّن البابا فرنسيس المطران باواي سورو ليقيم في أبرشية مار بطرس والمطران الفخري لمدينة فورتيانا.

**١ نيسان ٢٠١٥**: تمّ إنشاء دير الكلدان الجديد - دير مار يوسف - بانتماء كاهن واحد وراهبين. (سنة ٢٠١٧ تغيّر اسم الدير واصبح «أبناء العهد» عام ٢٠٢١ ضمّ ٧ رهبان كلدان).

**٧ أيار ٢٠١٦**: قَبِل الأب الأقدس استقالة المطران سرهد يوسب جمّو مطران كاتدرائية مار بطرس الرسول في سان دييغو «للكلدان، الولايات المتحدة الأمريكية، وعيّن المطران شليمون وردوني، مساعد بغداد للكلدان، مدبرا رسولياً.

**١٤ ايار ٢٠١٦**: وصل المطران شليمون وردوني إلى سان دييغو. واصبح هو المدبر الرسولي حتى تعيين المطران الجديد، المطران عمانوئيل شليطا.

**٧ تموز ٢٠١٧**: تمّ شراء كنيسة ثالثة وأرض مجاورة في سان دييغو - كنيسة القديس يوحنا الكلدانية الكاثوليكية. كانت قيمة الكنيسة ٥٦٠,٠٠٠ دولار وتمّ دفعها وتبرعت بها عائلة كلدانية تعيش في سان ديكو.

**٩ آب ٢٠١٧**: عيّن البابا فرنسيس مار عمانويل حنا شليطا أسقفاً جديداً لأبرشية القديس بطرس الرسول في سان دييغو.

**٢٥ آب ٢٠١٧**: وصل غبطة البطريرك لويس ساكو في أول زيارة رعوية له إلى أبرشية القديس بطرس الكلدانية الكاثوليكية. استمرت الزيارة الرعوية حتى ٩ سبتمبر ٢٠١٧.

عيّن البابا أسقفاً أبرشياً للقديس بطرس الرسول من سان دييغو للكلدان في الولايات المتحدة الأمريكية، المطران عمانويّل حنا شليطا، نقله من أبرشية مار أداي للكلدان في تورنتو في كندا الى سانديكو.

في الكهون. التحق خمسة شبان من كاتدرائية القديس بطرس بالمعهد الجديد.

**في ١٢ كانون الثاني (يناير) ٢٠٠٩:** انتقل المطران مار باواي سورو للإقامة في سان دييكو في مقر الأسقف مع المطران مار سرهد يوسب جمّو.

**١٦ كانون الثاني (يناير) ٢٠٠٩:** احتفلت كاتدرائية مار بطرس الكلدانية الكاثوليكية بالذكرى الخامسة والثلاثين لتأسيس أبرشية مار بطرس والذكرى الخامسة والعشرين (اليوبيل الفضي) لتكريس كنيسة مار بطرس.

ابرشية مار بطرس في سان دييكو

## الحاكم بيتر ددّه

تمَّ تعيين القاضي بيتر سي دده في المحكمة العليا لمقاطعة سان دييغو في يونيو ١٩٩٨ من قبل الحاكم بيت ويلسون. شغل منصب قاضي إشراف فرع المقاطعة الشرقية في محكمة الكهون العليا (٢٠٠٧-٢٠١١)، ورئيس لجنة الاستئناف (٢٠٠٧)، ورئيس المحكمة الجنائية لمحكمة سان دييغو العليا (٢٠٠١-٢٠٠٥) ومحكمة فيستا العليا (١٩٩٨-٢٠٠٠). بالإضافة إلى عمل القاضي ددّه في القضايا الجنائية، ترأس جلسات محكمة المشردين في قرية سانت فنسنت دي بول والمحاربين القدامى في فيتنام في ملجأ سانديكو للمشردين. قبل انضمامه إلى هيئة المحكمة العليا، كان نائب

بعد إنهاء دراسته في روما لفترة خمس عشرة سنة. عُيِّن راعياً لرعية القديس يوحنا المعمدان في بغداد، حيث كان يخدم من عام ١٩٦٩ إلى عام ١٩٧٤ بعده أصبح عميد المدرسة البطريركية الكلدانية. وفي تشرين الاول عام ١٩٧٧، أصبح راعياً مساعداً لرعية أم الله في ساوثفيلد، ميشيكان. ثم في عام ١٩٨٣، تم تعيينه راعياً لكنيسة القديس يوسف في تروي بولاية ميشيكان، حيث خدم حتى ترقيته إلى الأسقفية.

في عام ٢٠٠٢: أنشأ البابا يوحنا بولس الثاني أبرشية ثانية للكنيسة الكلدانية في الولايات المتحدة. ستقسم الأبرشية الجديدة البلاد بين الشرق والغرب. منح مار سرهد جمّو مقعدًا رسوليًا لرئاسة أبرشية مار بطرس الرسول التي تغطي غرب الولايات المتحدة. نال الرسامة الأسقفية ١٨ تموز ٢٠٠٢ ثم تمّ التنصيب الرسمي لابرشية سانيكو ٢٥ تموز ٢٠٠٢.

١٧ كانون الثاني ٢٠٠٣: تمّ تدشين دار الكهنة الجديد في كاتدرائية مار بطرس الكلدانية.

١٥ كانون الثاني ٢٠٠٤: تشير سجلات أبرشية مار بطرس إلى وجود ٢٠٧٥ عائلة كلدانية مسجلة.

١٥ كانون الثاني ٢٠٠٦: بلغ سكان كاتدرائية مار بطرس الكلدانية الكاثوليكية ٢٢٦٧ عائلة.

١٥ كنون الثاني ٢٠٠٧: اصبح سكان كاتدرائية مار بطرس الكلدانية الكاثوليكية ٢٦١٠ أسرة.

١٦ ايار ٢٠٠٧: قبل مار سرهد يوسب جمّو، في كاتدرائية مار بطرس، الوعود المؤقتة لثلاث فتيات، لجمعية العلمانيين المسماة «عمال الكرم» في إلكهون كاليفورنيا (تمّ غلق الجمعية ٢٠١٨).

٥ كانون الثاني ٢٠٠٨: بلغ سكان كاتدرائية مار بطرس الكلدانية الكاثوليكية ٢٨٥٦ عائلة تضم ٧,٣٨٣ من أبناء الرعية.

٢٣ تموز ٢٠٠٨: أصبحت السيدة يولي هيشا شمعون، ٤٢ سنة، أول قاضية كلدانية في ولاية كاليفورنيا وتم تعيينها في المحكمة العليا في مقاطعة سان دييغو.

٢٥ تموز ٢٠٠٨: افتتح مار سرهد يوسب جمّو معهد – سمنير مار أبا الكبير

**في تشرين الثاني ١٩٨٩:** حسب دليل أبرشية القديس بطرس الجديد، بلغ عدد العوائل المسجلة ٧٤٠.

**٣ تشرين الأول ١٩٩٣:** اصبح سكان أبرشية القديس بطرس ١٠٧٨ عائلة مع ٤٩٦٤ من أبناء الرعية يملكون ٦٠٦ مشروعاً.

**١٥ أيلول ١٩٩٤:** اصبح سكان القديس بطرس ١١٩٧ عائلة تضم ٥,٥٧١ فرداً.

**١٥ تشرين الثاني ١٩٩٦:** بلغ العدد الإجمالي للأسر المسجلة ١٣٣٥ أسرة. كان هناك ٦٨٩ عائلة لديها عمل واحد و١٠٢ عائلة لديها عملان أو أكثر.

**١٩ حزيران ١٩٩٨:** أدى السيد بيتر ددّه اليمين الدستورية كأول قاضٍ كلداني في المحكمة العليا في مقاطعة سان ديكو. وفي الأول من كانون الثاني (يناير) ٢٠٠٨، تم تعيين السيد بيتر ددّه رئيساً للمحكمة العليا في الكاهون.

**٣ تشرين الأول ١٩٩٩:** أشارت سجلات أبرشية مار بطرس إلى أن هناك ١٨٢١ عائلة كلدانية مسجلة بإجمالي ٩,١٠٥ فرد.

**٦ تشرين الاول ١٩٩٩: تم تكريس كنيسة خورنة مار ميخا. وتعيين القس صبري قجبو كأول راعي للخورنة الثانية للكلدان في إلكهون تحت اسم كنيسة مار ميخا الكلدانية الكاثوليكية.**

**٢١ أيار ٢٠٠٢:** أصبحت كنيسة مار بطرس الكلدانية الكاثوليكية في إلكهون بكاليفورنيا مقراً للأبرشية الكلدانية الثانية في الولايات المتحدة. وسميت كاتدرائية مار بطرس الكلدانية الكاثوليكية. عين الأب الأقدس، البابا يوحنا بولس الثاني، القس الكلداني سرهد يوسب جمّو، كأول أسقف للأبرشية المنشأة حديثاً. تم تنصيبه في ٢٥ يوليو ٢٠٠٢، وانتهت مدة ادارته للابرشية بتقاعده في ٧ مايو ٢٠١٦.

ولد مار سرهد يوسيب هرمز جمّو في بغداد في ١٤ آذار (مارس) ١٩٤١. دخل سمنير معهد شمعون الصفا الموصل. غادر إلى روما في سن السابعة عشرة. التحق بالجامعة البابوية Urbaniana، حيث حصل على درجة الماجستير في كل من الفلسفة واللاهوت. رُسم كاهنًا في ١٩ كانون الأول (ديسمبر) ١٩٦٤، وتابع دراسات الدكتوراه في المعهد البابوي الشرقي حيث نال شهادة الدكتوراه. في الدراسات الكنسية الشرقية. كانت أطروحته بعنوان «هيكلية القداس الكلداني». درّس في المعهد الشرقي البابوي

**١٠ ايلول ١٩٨٣**: تم تكريس مبنى كنيسة مار بطرس حسب الطقوس الكلدانية الشرقية الكاثوليكية .

**٥ كانون الثاني ١٩٨٤**: بلغ عدد العوائل المسجلة في الخورنة ٤٩٥عائلة.

**١ أيلول ١٩٨٥** تمّ تعيين القس ميخائيل بزّي مساعداً في خورنة مار بطرس في الكهون. ثمّ في ٢٥ نيسان ١٩٨٦ منح المطران ابراهيم إبراهيم للقس ميخائيل السماح لان يشارك القس كتولا في ادارة الخورنة.

**كانون الأول (ديسمبر) ١٩٨٥**: بلغ عدد العوائل المسجلة في الخورنة ٥٤٩ عائلة كلدانية.

**١٠ كانون الثاني ١٩٨٦**: تمّ إنشاء الأنشطة التالية في كنيسة القديس بطرس: أخوية الكتاب المقدس للكبار (٤٠ عضواً)، دراسة الكتاب المقدس لطلاب الكلية والخريجين (٥٣ عضواً)، الجوقة (١٥ عضواً)، مدرسة التعليم المسيحي: مرحلة التمهيدي حتى الصف الثامن (٢٧٠) قام بتدريس الطلاب ١٨ معلماً كلدانياً، وفصل المدرسة الثانوية (٣٠ طالباً)، والدراسة الآرامية الكلاسيكية (١٦ طالباً). بدأت فرقة الانشاد باللغة الإنكليزية، المكونة من ١٢ عضواً. عام ١٩٨٧ تأسست أخوية القلب المقدس وضمّت ٥٥ عضواً. لقد تمّ إنشاء هذه الأنشطة من قبل القس ميخائيل بزّي بعد ثلاثة أشهر من تعيينه في خورنة مار بطرس الكلدانية في سان ديكو.

**٢٠ ذار ١٩٨٧**: توفي القس بطرس كتولا . مؤسس خورنة مار بطرس والذي خدم المجتمع الكلداني في سان دييغو كراعٍ لمدة ١٤ عاماً.

**وفي ٢٧ آذار ١٩٨٧**: تم تنصيب القس ميخائيل بزّي راعيا لخورنة مار بطرس في سانديكو.

**١٥ كانون الأول ١٩٨٧**: اصبح سكان خورنة مار بطرس الكلدانية الكاثوليكية ٦٠٠ عائلة تضم ما مجموعه ٣٠٠٠ فرداً.

**٢٥ كانون الثاني ١٩٨٨**: اشارت إحصائيات أبرشية القديس بطرس إلى وجود ٨٠٠ عائلة كلدانية مسجلة تضم ٤,٠٠٠ فرداً.

**٢٨ كانون الثاني ١٩٨٨**: باشرت الخورنة ببناء القاعة الكبرى. وتمّ افتتاحها رسمياً في ٢٩ تشرين الثاني ١٩٨٩.

**حزيران ١٩٧٧:** بلغ عدد العوائل المسجلة ٢٢٠ عائلة كلدانية.

**٩ تشرين الأول ١٩٧٨:** وصل القس إبراهيم إبراهيم (حالياً الأسقف الفخري لأبرشية القديس توما الكلدانية) من بغداد للمساعدة في أبرشية مار بطرس. خدم مع القس كتولا، من ١٩ تشرين الأول ١٩٧٨ إلى ١ كانون الثاني ١٩٧٩، غادر بعدها إلى لوس أنجلوس وأسّس خورنة جديدة باسم خورنة مار بولس.

**٢٩ حزيران ١٩٧٩:** احتفلت أبرشية مار بطرس بوضع حجر الأساس للكنيسة الجديدة. وفي نفس اليوم، نشرت الخورنة النسخة الثانية من دليلها. بلغ عدد العائلات المسجلة ١١٩٠ عائلة كلدانية.

**تشرين الثاني ١٩٨١:** وصلت راهبتان كلدانيتان بنات مريم المحبول بها بلا دنس من بغداد بالعراق لخدمة أبرشية القديس بطرس.

**٢٦ كانون الثاني ١٩٨٢:** أنشأ قداسة البابا القديس يوحنا بولس الثاني إكسرخية مار توما في ٧ آذار ١٩٨٢ وعُين الأسقف إبراهيم إبراهيم كأول أسقف للإكسارخية الجديدة. رفع البابا يوحنا بولس الثاني الإكسارخية الرسولية للكلدان في الولايات المتحدة إلى رتبة أبرشية في ٣ آب ١٩٨٥.

**وفي ايار ٢٠١٤** عيّن قداسة البابا فرنسيس القس فرانك قلابات أسقفاً جديدا لأبرشية مار توما الرسول الكلدانية – مشيكن خلفا للمطران مار أبراهيم أبراهيم الذي قدّم استقالته لبلوغه سن التقاعد وتمت رسامة الاسقف الجديد (مار فرنسيس قلابات) في ١٥ حزيران ٢٠١٤ في كاتدرائية ام الله – ديترويت.

كانت خورنة مار بطرس جزءاً من الأبرشية حتى ٢١ ايار ٢٠٠٢، عندما أصبحت كنيسة القديس بطرس الكلدانية الكاثوليكية في الكهون، كاليفورنيا مقراً للأبرشية الكلدانية الثانية – أبرشية القديس بطرس الرسول الكلدانية في الولايات المتحدة.

**أيار ١٩٨٢- ٣٠ أيلول ١٩٨٢:** تم تشييد أول كنيسة في رانجو سان ديكو وبيت الكاهن القديم.

**٨ تشرين الثاني ١٩٨٢- ٢٩ حزيران ١٩٨٤:** تمّ تشييد كنيسة القديس بطرس في الكهون.

**٥ كانون الثاني ١٩٨٣:** بلغ عدد العوائل المسجلة في الخورنة ٤١١ عائلة.

تزوج ماري لين دريك وسرعان ما انتقلوا إلى تشولا فيستا. أصبح ابنهما، بيتر، رئيساً لقاضي المحكمة العليا في سانديكو ١٩٩٣. انضم دّده، وهو ديمقراطي، إلى حملة الرئيس جون إف كينيدي وأصبح مدرّساً للعلوم السياسية في كلية مجتمع قبل أن يبدأ ترشحه لمنصب الرئاسة. خدم في المجلس التشريعي للولاية لأكثر من ٢٥ عاماً، ثم ترشح لاحقاً (دون جدوى) للكونغرس لكنه لم ينجح. خدم في ساكرامنتو لسنوات عديدة في لجنة الإيرادات والضرائب. توفي عن عمر يناهز ٩٨، ٣٠ أغسطس، ٢٠١٩. سُمّي مبنى مكاتب الدولة على اسم دّده، الذي أصبح يعرف باسم والد كالترانس.

**حزيران ١٩٦٠:** وصل السيد صليوا سمعان من بغداد لزيارة سان ديكو. وجد حوالي ١٠ عوائل كلدانية تعيش فيها.

**٦ كانون الأول ١٩٧٣:** تم تأسيس أول خورنة كلدانية كاثوليكية وتمّ تعيين القس الكلداني بطرس كتولا كاهنا لها. في ذلك الوقت كان عدد العائلات ٧٠ عائلة كلدانية في سان ديكو.

**آذار ١٩٧٤:** حسب أول تعداد خاص لرعية مار بطرس، كان عدد المسجلين ١١٧ عائلة كلدانية.

**نيسان ١٩٧٤:** قرر القس كتولا ومجلس الرعية تسمية الخورنة الجديدة باسم مار بطرس الكلدانية الكاثوليكية في سان ديكو.

**٢٠ ايار ١٩٧٤:** اشترت خورنة مار بطرس الكلدانية ٥,٠٩ فداناً من الأرض مقابل ٤٨,٣٥٥ دولاراً في رانجو سان دييكو؛ الموقع الحالي للكنيسة. تمّ تسديد الدفعة النهائية لهذه الأرض في ١٠ يونيو ١٩٧٩ وبلغ إجماليها ٥٦,٤٤٢ دولاراً. (من ١٩٨٣ إلى ٢٠٠٣، توسعت الرعية لتشمل كنيسة مار بطرس، وقاعة اجتماعية – دينية وقاعة قديمة).

**٢٠ حزيران ١٩٧٤:** وصل القس ميخائيل بزّي من روما لزيارة سان ديكو. في ذلك الوقت، كان سكان أبرشية مار بطرس ١٣٠ عائلة مسجلة.

**١٥ نيسان ١٩٧٥:** نشرت رعية مار بطرس دليلها الأول. كان عدد السكان المسجلين ١٥٠ عائلة كلدانية في سان ديكو.

# الفصل السادس
# الكلدان الكاثوليك في سان دييكو

إن الغالبية العظمى من الكلدان في سان دييغو تعود جذورهم إلى محافظة نينوى في شمال بلاد ما بين النهرين (العراق). ترك هؤلاء الكلدان بلادهم باحثين عن حياة أفضل ويأملون في جو أكثر هدوءاً وسلاماً.

اعتباراً من تشرين الأول ٢٠٠٩، كان سكان كاتدرائية القديس بطرس يتألفون من ٢٤٥٧ عائلة، مع ١١,٤٥١ من الكلدان المسجلين حالياً.

عام ٢٠١٧ قُدّر عدد الكلدان الكاثوليك في سان ديكو بـ ٠٠٠,٤٠ الفا.

فيما يلي مراحل تاريخية مهمة لهجرة الكلدان إما من ديترويت – ميشيكان أو مباشرة من بلاد ما بين النهرين – العراق إلى سان ديكو.

كانون الأول ١٩٥١: كان أول مهاجر كلداني إلى سانديكو هو الدكتور جوزيف جبران جاء للبحث الطبي واستقرّ. وبعده باشر المهاجرون ينتقلون إلى المدينة.

في شهر آب ١٩٥٤: وصل السيد رمزي أليكس توماس من بغداد للدراسة في جامعة ولاية سان دييكو. بعد أن أكمل دراسته، افتتح شركته الخاصة، مبيعات قطع غيار السيارات المستعملة.

حزيران ١٩٥٥: قام السيد والسيدة عزيز حبيب بزيارة مدينة سان دييكو لمدة أسبوعين من ديترويت. في يوليو ١٩٥٧، انتقلوا إلى سان دييغو. كانوا أول الكلدان الذين افتتحوا أول محل للبقالة.

### السناتور وديع ددّه

حزيران ١٩٥٩: انتقل السيد والسيدة وديع ددّه من ديترويت إلى سان دييغو. جاء السناتور وديع ددّه إلى أمريكا من العراق في الأربعينيات من القرن الماضي، وأصبح مدرساً ثم خدم لاحقاً في جمعية كاليفورنيا من عام ١٩٦٧ إلى عام ١٩٨٣ وفي مجلس شيوخ الولاية من عام ١٩٨٣ إلى ١٩٩٣. وصل أخيراً إلى أمريكا، وعاش لأول مرة في ديترويت، حيث درس القانون الدستوري والعلوم السياسية.

أنشأ البابا يوحنا بولس الثاني ابرشية مار بطرس الجديدة بناءً على طلب أساقفة الكنيسة الكلدانية، وهي تشمل الولايات التسع عشرة التالية: أريزونا، ألاسكا، كاليفورنيا، كولورادو، هاواي، أيداهو، كانزاس، مونتانا، نبراسكا، نيفادا، أوكلاهوما، نيو مكسيكو وداكوتا الشمالية وداكوتا الجنوبية وأوريجون وتكساس ويوتا وواشنطن ووايومنك.

عيّن الأب الأقدس كاهناً كلدانياً القس سرهد يوسب جمّو كأول أسقف للأبرشية المنشأة حديثاً. ولد المطران سرهد في بغداد بالعراق عام ١٩٤١، وسيم أسقفاً في ١٨ تموز ٢٠٠٢ في تروي بولاية ميشكن. في ٢٥ تموز (يوليو) ٢٠٠٢، وتم تنصيب الأسقف سرهد يوسب كأول مطران لأبرشية مار بطرس الرسول الكلدانية الكاثوليكية ومقر الأبرشية كاتدرائية مار بطرس الكلدانية الكاثوليكية في سان دييكو، كاليفورنيا.١٥ كانون الثاني ٢٠٠٨ الانظمام الى الكنيسة الكلدانية الكاثوميكية:

في الفترة بين كانون الثاني وشهر أيار ٢٠٠٨ التحق بالكنيسة الكلدانية الكاثوليكية المطران مار بأواي سورو و٦ كهنة و٣٠ شمامسا و٥,٠٠٠ مؤمن رسمياً بالكنيسة الكلدانية الكاثوليكية، أربع رعايا وبعثتان في كاليفورنيا. (كانوا ينتمون سابقاً إلى الكنيسة الآشورية الشرقية).

إحدى عشرة خورنة وثلاث إرساليات. الأبرشيات الإحدى عشرة هي:
١- كاتدرائية القديس بطرس (إلكهون، كاليفورنيا).
٢- سانت مايكل (إلكهون، كاليفورنيا).
٣- سانت بولس (شمال هوليوود، كاليفورنيا).
٤- سانت جورج (سانتا آنا، كاليفورنيا).
٥- سانت توماس (تورلوك، كاليفورنيا).
٦- سانت ماري (كامبل، كاليفورنيا).
٧- مار أوراها (سكوتسديل، أريزونا).
٨- سانتا بربارا (لاس فيكاس، نيفادا).
٩- القديس ماثيو (سيريس، كاليفورنيا).
١٠- سيدة المساعدة الدائمة (ساكرامنتو، كاليفورنيا).
١١- مار يوحنا الحبيب (إلكهون، كاليفورنيا).

في ٢٦ كانون الثاني ١٩٨٢، أنشأ قداسة البابا يوحنا بولس الثاني إكسرخسية رسولية للمؤمنين الكلدان المقيمين في الولايات المتحدة، وعيّن القس إبراهيم إبراهيم كأول رئيس رسولي. في ٧ آذار عام ١٩٨٢، رُسم القس إبراهيم أسقفاً في بغداد وتمّ تنصيبه كأول أسقف للإكسارسية الجديدة. رفع البابا يوحنا بولس الثاني الإكسارسية الرسولية للكلدان في الولايات المتحدة إلى رتبة أبرشية في ٣ آب ١٩٨٥. وكان اللقب الرسمي لهذه الأبرشية هو أبرشية القديس توما الرسول الكلدانية. أقام مار إبراهيم إبراهيم في مدينة ديترويت بولاية ميشكن، ومقر هذه الأبرشية كاتدرائية أم الله الكاثوليكية.

وفي أيار ٢٠١٤ عيّن قداسة البابا فرنسيس القس فرانك قلابات أسقفاً جديداً لأبرشية مار توما الرسول الكلدانية – مشيكن خلفا للمطران مار أبراهيم إبراهيم الذي قدّم استقالته لبلوغه سن التقاعد وتمت رسامة الأسقف الجديد (مار فرنسيس قلابات) في ١٥ حزيران ٢٠١٤ في كاتدرائية أم الله – ديترويت.

في ٢١ أيار ٢٠٠٢، أصبحت كنيسة القديس بطرس الكلدانية الكاثوليكية في إلكهون بكاليفورنيا مقر الأبرشية الكلدانية الثانية في الولايات المتحدة، وأطلق عليها اسم كاتدرائية القديس بطرس الكلدانية الكاثوليكية.

# الفصل الخامس
# الكنيسة الكلدانية في الولايات المتحدة

وصل الرواد الأوائل للشعب الكلداني إلى الولايات المتحدة في نهاية القرن التاسع عشر. كانت الفئة الأولى قليلة العدد، ولكن بحلول منتصف القرن العشرين، كان هناك كثيرون منتشرون في جميع أنحاء البلاد اعتباراً من ٢٥ تموز ٢٠٠٢، توجد أبرشيتان للكلدان الكاثوليك داخل الولايات المتحدة الأمريكية:

١- أبرشية مار توما الرسول الكلدانية الكاثوليكية، تضمّ الولايات الشرقية.

٢- أبرشية مار بطرس الرسول الكلدانية الكاثوليكية، تضم الولايات الغربية.

يقع مقر أبرشية القديس توما الرسول الكلدانية في متروبولتان ديترويت، ميشيغان. وهي تغطي إحدى وثلاثين ولاية في شرق الولايات المتحدة، وتضم أكثر من مائة وعشرين ألف عضو في اثني عشر خورنات. الرعايا الاثنتا عشرة هي:

١- كاتدرائية ام الله (ساوثفيلد، ميشيكان).

٢- القلب الاقدس (وارن، ميشيكان).

٣- مار أدّاي (أوك بارك، ميشيكان).

٤- سانت جوزيف (تروي ميشيكان).

٥- سانت توماس (وست بلومفيلد، ميشيكان).

٦- سانت جورج (بلدة شيلبي، ميشيكان).

٧- خورنة الشهداء القديسين (ستيرلنج هايتس، ميشيكان).

٨- سيدة العون الدائم (وارن ، ميشيكان).

٩- هولي كروس (فارمنكتون هيلز، ميشكان).

١٠- سانت بول (غراند بلانك، ميشيكان).

١١- سانت إفريم (شيكاغو، إيلينوي).

١٢- مارت مريم (شيكاغو، إيلينوي).

يقع مقر الأبرشية الثانية مار بطرس الرسول الكلدانية الكاثوليكية في سانديكو، كاليفورنيا. وهي تغطي تسع عشرة ولاية غربية تضم أكثر من سبعين ألف عضو في

وراهبات القلب المقدس الكلدانيات. وفي سانديكو يوجد دير للرهبان يضمّ ٧ شباب. وكذلك في سانديكو اكليريكية تضم ٥ شباب.

١٦ أيار ٢٠٠٧ بدأ دير كلداني للفتيات سمّاه سيادة المطران سرهد جمّو «فعلة الكرم» في سان دييكو، كاليفورنيا. (توقف الدير عام ٢٠١٨).

# الفصــل الرابــع
# الكنيســة الكلدانيــة في العالــم

تتكون الكنيسة الكلدانية من مسيحيي الشرق الأوسط الذين يستخدمون الآرامية كلغة أم. وهي واحدة من اثنتين وعشرين كنيسة ذات طقوس شرقية معترف بها من قبل الكرسي الرسولي في روما.

الكلدان كاثوليك متحدون مع روما، رغم أنهم ليسوا من الرومان الكاثوليك. إنهم واحد في الإيمان مع روما، لكنهم مختلفون في العادات (الطقوس). على سبيل المثال، تختلف طقوسهم، على الرغم من أن لديهم نفس الأسرار. يقدمون سرّ الميرون لأطفالهم مباشرة بعد تعميدهم. بعض كهنتهم متزوجون، إلّا أن معظم الكهنة الكلدان يعتنقون العزوبة الاختيارية. لديهم أساقفتهم، الذين يشكلون تسلسلاً هرمياً مستقلاً عن الأساقفة الرومان. ومع ذلك، فإن البطريرك الذي يقود الكنيسة الكلدانية يخضع لسلطة البابا.

دُعي البطريرك الكلداني بطريرك بابل، ولكن مجمع الأساقفة الكلدان في شهر آب ٢٠٢١ غيّر الاسم إلى «بطريرك الكلدان» ويقيم في بغداد بالعراق. ينتشر اتباعه من الكلدان في جميع أنحاء العالم ويبلغ عددهم حوالي مليونين منهم ٥٠,٠٠٠ يقيمون داخل العراق وحوالي ٢٥٠,٠٠٠ في الولايات المتحدة والباقي منتشر في جميع أنحاء العالم.

وفقاً لتعداد الكنائس لعام ٢٠٠٨، كانت هناك ثمانية أبرشيات كلدانية وتسع أبرشيات، مع ثمانية عشر أسقفاً. كانت توجد حوالي مائة واثني عشر ابرشية وعشر إرساليات يخدمها ما يقرب من مائة وعشرة كهنة.

منذ عام ٢٠٠٣، يتعرض الكلدان الكاثوليك للاضطهاد في العراق، وخاصة في بغداد والموصل. استشهد العديد من رجال الدين والعديد من الأبرشيات شبه مغلقة، مما أجبر رعاتهم على اللجوء إلى أي منطقة توفر لهم ملاذاً آمناً، إما إلى مدن أخرى في شمال العراق أو مغادرة البلاد معاً.

هناك رهبانية واحدة من الرجال وإكليريكية واحدة مع طلاب اللاهوت والفلسفة يستعدون للكهنوت. هناك رهبنتان للنساء في بغداد، بنات مريم الطاهرة الكلدانيات

روما واعتنق الإيمان الكاثوليكي أمام البابا يوليوس الثالث عام ١٥٥٣. ومع ذلك، بحلول عام ١٥٩٢، فإن معظم الكاثوليك في بلاد ما بين النهرين قد انفصلوا مرة أخرى عن روما. لكن بشكل دوري اتحدت مجموعات مختلفة منهم مع روما فقط لقطع العلاقات مرة أخرى بعد بضع سنوات. ولكن بحلول القرن التاسع عشر، فاق عدد الكاثوليك الذين تم توحيدهم عدداً، على الرغم من أن بعضهم كان لا يزال منفصلاً.

الكلدان، موجودون منذ آلاف السنين قبل المسيح ولكن كدولة، هم موجودون منذ القرنين السابع والسادس قبل الميلاد. والكلدان اليوم هم من نسل تلك الأمة العظيمة. إن مصطلح «الكنيسة الكلدانية» استخدم عام ١٤٤٥ م من قبل البابا أوجينيوس الخامس معترفا باصطلاحات الشعب لتمييز أتباع كنيسة المشرق في قبرص، الذين تصالحوا حديثًا مع روما، عن أولئك الذين لم يتصالحوا. من المهم أن نلاحظ أن الشعب الكلداني قد انتشر وعاش في العراق وفي جميع أنحاء الشرق الأوسط لآلاف السنين. وعندما اعترف البابا بمجموعة صغيرة من الكلدان الذين يعيشون في قبرص باسم «الكنيسة الكلدانية»، لم يخلق اسماً لهم. وبدلاً من ذلك، أكّد وأعلن عن أصلهم وأقرّ بأن آخر حكام بلاد ما بين النهرين الأصليين كانوا في الواقع من الكلدان، وأنه منذ سقوطهم في أيدي الفرس عام ٥٣٩ قبل الميلاد، كان العراق يحكمه أجانب. وهكذا، يظل الكلدان هم الشعب الأصلي للعراق، خلافاً لما يدعيه بعض الذين يعتقدون أن الاسم «الكلداني» ظهر في القرن الخامس عشر الميلادي. ونحن نلاحظ ان الذين هاجروا من كنيسة المشرق إلى قبرص أعلنوا الهوية الكلدانية تعبيراً عن ذاتهم التاريخية فاحترمت الكنيسة اللاتينية هذا الواقع.

# الفصل الثالث
## الكنيسة الكلدانية

منذ نهاية القرن الأول للميلاد، ازدهرت المسيحية في بلاد ما بين النهرين بين أحفاد الأمتين العظيمتين والقديمتين الكلدانية والآشورية. بمجرد قبولهما المسيحية، فضّلت الامّتان اسم «المسيحية» على أسمائهما القومية القديمة. هذه الكنيسة، التي تألفت من هاتين الأمتين، كانت تسمى «كنيسة المشرق» لانها كانت شرق الامبراطورية الرومانيه وكان نهر الفرات الحد الفاصل بينهما. ازدهرت الكنيسة في بلاد ما بين النهرين وتوسعت في بلدان كل من كلدو وآشور وفارس والجزيرة العربية ومنغوليا في آسيا وساحل مالابار في الهند وحتى الصين.

خلال القرون الخمسة الأولى بعد الميلاد، كانت الكنيسة الكلدانية والآشورية في شركة مع الكنيسة الرومانية الكاثوليكية. حتى أنه تم إنشاء مدرسة للتعليم المسيحي في مدينة إديسا (أورفة الحالية - الرها). وصلت هذه المدرسة إلى أعلى درجات مجدها في عهد مار أبريم (القديس أفرام) عام ٣٦٣ بعد الميلاد، ومع ذلك، أعلنت كنيسة الشرق حكمها الذاتي عن روما، عندما أصبحت نصيبين المركز الفكري الجديد لبلاد ما بين النهرين بمرسوم إمبراطوري.

أُطلق على رأس كنيسة المشرق الجالس في بلاد ما بين النهرين لقب «كاثوليكوس» أي الاب العام او الجامع. عام ٤٢٤ م أعلن مجمع داديشوع ان جاثاليق المشرق هو المرجعية الأخيرة للكنيسة. أقام في سلوقية - قطيسفون، قرب بغداد، العراق. في القرن السابع، غزا المسلمون بلاد ما بين النهرين. في عام ٧٨٠ م، نقل الكاثوليكوس تيميثيوس مقر إقامته إلى العاصمة بغداد. بحلول نهاية القرن العاشر الميلادي، كان هناك خمسة عشر ابرشية لكنيسة المشرق في بلاد ما بين النهرين، وخمس ابرشيات خارج حدودها بما في ذلك تلك الموجودة في إيران وسوريا ومصر والهند والصين. امتدت ابرشيات الكنيسة هذه إلى شرق سيبيريا ومنغوليا.

حدثت محاولة من جانب كنيسة المشرق في بلاد ما بين النهرين للالتحاق بالكنيسة الكاثوليكية وتحققت عندما ذهب رئيس الدير الذي انتخب بطريركا يوحنا سولاقا إلى

٦- المغول ٢٥٨-١٣٥٦ م.
٧- أسرة الجليرد ١٣٥٦-١٤١٠ م.
٨- التركمان ١٤١٠-١٥٠٩م.
٩- الفترة الأولى للأتراك العثمانيين ١٥٣٤-١٦٢١ م.
١٠- الفترة الثانية للفُرس ١٦٢١-١٦٣٨ م.
١١- الفترة الثانية للأتراك العثمانيين ١٦٣٨-١٩١٦ م.
١٢- استولى البريطانيون، بقيادة الجنرال مود بمساعدة الهنود، على العاصمة بغداد عام ١٩١٧ م.
١٣- منذ عام ١٩٢١ الى ١٩٥٨م، تعاقَب ملوك العرب على الحكم.
١٤- عام ١٩٥٨م أصبح العراق جمهورية.

القانونية والتجارية بأعداد كبيرة على تكوين صورة كاملة للحياة في الإمبراطورية البابلية الجديدة (الكلدانية). ربما لخّص النبي إرميا (٥١: ٧) أفضل تلخيص للحكم الكلداني في وصفه لبابل الكلدانيين على أنها «كأس ذهبي في يد الرب تسكر كل الأرض» كما وصف حبقوق النبي (١: ٦-١١) الكلدانيين «هكذا قال الرب: أنا أقيم الكلدانيين الشعب الذي يسير في عرض الأرض أسرع من النمور هي خيولهم وخيولهم أكثر حرصاً من الذئاب في المساء. خيلهم تقفز وفرسانهم يأتون من بعيد. يطيرون كالنسر مسرعاً بالابتلاع. يأتي كل منهما من الشرق، وبداية ظهورهما المشترك هي رياح عاصفة تتراكم على الأسرى مثل الرمل. يسخرون من الملوك والأمراء هم أضحوكة. يضحكون على أي حصن، يكدسون منحدرًا ويغزونه. ثم ينحرفون مثل الريح ويعبروا».

بعد سقوط بابل في أيدي الفرس، قام الكلدان بالعديد من المحاولات للعودة إلى السلطة، لكن لم تنجح أي منها. سجّل المؤرخون ثلاث حركات تمرد رئيسية بقيادة الكلدان: الأولى حدثت في ٥٢٢-٥٢١ ق م. عندما استولى نيدونتا بل، أو نبوكذنصر الثالث، على العرش في بابل. قُتل بعد ذلك بوقت قصير، وفشلت الحركة. الثانية التي حدثت عام ٥٢١ ق. م. عندما قاد الجنرال الكلداني، نبوكذنصر الرابع، ثورة فاشلة وتم إعدامه. والثالثة كانت عندما قام الكلدان الآخرون ببذل جهد لاستعادة السلطة في بابل. قاد بلشيماني وشمسة عريب تمردًا عام ٤٨٢ ق. م، لكنهما قتلا. بعد هذا الوقت، استمر الكلدانيون في التجول في بلاد ما بين النهرين مع إخوتهم الآشوريين. كلاهما يمثلان حضارة عمرها آلاف السنين.

ان سقوط نينوى عام ٦١٢ ق. م. وبابل عام ٥٣٩ ق. م. شهد تراجع حضارة بلاد ما بين النهرين ونهاية آخر سلالة حاكمة أصلية في بلاد ما بين النهرين، سيطر الغزاة الأجانب على بلاد ما بين النهرين على التوالي من ٥٣٩ ق. م حتى ١٩٥٨م.

١- الفرس الأخمينيون ٥٣٩-٣٣٥ ق. م.

٢- الإغريق ٣٣١-١٣٠ ق. م.

٣- الفرثيون ١٣٠-٢٢٦ ق. م.

٤- الساسانيون الفُرس ٢٢٦-٦٣٦ م.

٥- العرب ٦٣٦-١٢٥٨ م.

المنفي، وأطلق سراحه من الحبس ورفعه فوق الملوك الأسرى الآخرين، وسمح له بتناول العشاء على المائدة الملكية (٢ ملوك ٢٥:٢٧ وإرميا ٥٢:٣١).

## ٤- نيريكلاصر (٥٥٩- ٥٥٦ ق.م)

وفقاً لسفر إرميا (٣٩: ٣-١٣)، إن ابنه لاباشي مردوخ قد قُتل وهو طفل. لا يُعرف سوى القليل عن عهده بخلاف حقيقة أنه أعاد ترميم معابد بابل وبورسيبا. كما قام بحملة في عام ٥٥٧ قبل الميلاد. ضد قيليقيا. توفي نيريكلاصر عام ٥٥٦ قبل الميلاد في ظروف مشكوك فيها.

## ٥ - نبونيدوس (٥٥٥-٥٣٩ ق.م)

كان نابونيدوس آخر ملوك بابل المستقلة. كان متعصباً دينياً، من أصل آرامي من حاران، وكان في الستينيات من عمره قبل أن يتولى عرش بابل. يبدو أنه قد تأثر بشدة بوالدته، أدا جوبي، كاهنة معبد الإله «سين» في حاران. هذا التأثير جعله يستبدل عبادة مردوك ونابو بإله القمر سين. بسبب الصراع مع الكهنة في بابل، نقل نابونيدوس مقر إقامته إلى شمال شبه الجزيرة العربية. بعد أن حاصر الجوف، ٢٨٠ ميلاً شرق العقبة، استقر في تيماء، الواحة الكبيرة في غرب شبه الجزيرة العربية. هناك كان بإمكانه أن يتجول بسهولة من واحة إلى اخرى حتى يثرب (المدينة). لمدة عشر سنوات، ظل نبونيدوس بعيداً عن العاصمة بابل. خلال هذا الوقت، ترك الحكومة في يد ابنه بيلشاصر، وهو جندي مقتدر، لكنه سياسي فقير. تعرضت سلطة بلشازار لتحدي من خلال التأثير المتزايد للفرس.

في سن السبعين، عاد نبونيدوس إلى بابل، لكن حياته المهنية لم تدم طويلاً. كان كاهن مردوخ، في بابل، قد انحاز إلى القائد الفارسي كورش، الذي أقام علاقات أفضل معه. هاجم قورش بابل في خريف عام ٥٣٩ ق.م. وانتصر على نبونيدوس ودخل مدينة بابل دون نزاع. من أجل استسلامه، حصل نابونيدوس على منطقة صغيرة في بلاد فارس.

كان هذا بمثابة نهاية آخر سلالة حاكمة محلية في بابل. لكن حُكم الملوك الكلدان ترك بصمة عميقة في تاريخ هذه المنطقة. ساعدتنا النقوش على الآثار والمراسلات والوثائق

فرعون هوفرا وعُزل من عرشه، وفي الفترة (٥٦٩-٥٣٦ ق. م)، احتل الجيش البابلي مصر.

غزا نبوكذنصر الثاني لبنان حيث أقيم له نقشاً منقوراً في وادي بريصا ليس بعيداً عن نهر الكلب. يُظهر هذا النقش نبوكذنصر الثاني وهو يقاتل أسداً والنقش يشير إلى رعايته لشعب لبنان.

يُعرِّف التاريخ نبوكذنصر الثاني على أنه باني مدينة بابل العظيمة والرائعة بجدرانها ذات اللون الوردي وشوارعها والمواكب العريضة والطوب الأزرق المحدب المزين بالتتين الأحمر والأسود والثيران البرية. وقام ببناء جدار دفاعي عظيم، جدار الوسط، شمال المدينة، كان هذا. الجدار المصمم لصد الغزاة البربريين، كان علو جداره يزيد عن ١٠٠ قدم، بنى نبوكذنصر الثاني «حديقة بابل المعلقة». تسمى حدائق بابل المعلقة أو جنائن بابل المعلقة عبارة عن تل اصطناعي **بناه لزوجته أميتيز، ابنة ملك ميديس**، التي جاءت من مقاطعة جبلية ووجدت صعوبة في التكيف مع سهول بلاد ما بين النهرين. تمّ وضع حدائق وبساتين ترفيهية مروية على طول هذه المدرجات. مع تبخر المياه المستخدمة للري، تمتص الحرارة من الكهوف التي تم تجويفها تحت المصاطب. وبالتالي، يمكن استخدام الكهوف للتخزين البارد.

قام نبوكذنصر الثاني بترميم مدينة بابل وجعلها واحدة من اجمل عجائب العالم، وقام أيضاً بحفر القنوات وبناء البحيرات وخزاناً كبيراً يحيط بالمدينة. وبالنسبة لمواد البناء، استخدم طوباً مع الإسفلت والطين. في وقت لاحق، تمّ استبدال الجير بالملاط (الطين الذي يطلى به الحائط). جنبا إلى جنب مع تجميل المقام الملكي، أنهى برج القواطع السبعة في بورسيبا.

توفي نبوكذنصر الثاني عام ٥٦٢ ق م. بعد بناء إمبراطورية كلدانية امتدت من البحر الأبيض المتوسط إلى الخليج الفارسي.

## ٣- أوّيـل مـردوخ: أي رجـل مـردوخ (٥٦٢-٥٥٩ ق. م)

خلف مرودخ والده نبوكذنصر الثاني، لكن حكمه لم يدم طويلا. تم طرده من عرشه واغتيل على يد صهره نيريجليسور. إلى جانب عدم شعبيته لدى كهنة بابل، لا يُعرف سوى القليل عن أويل مرودخ. يبدو أنه أظهر تساهلاً مع يهوياقيم، ملك يهودا

في نفس العام، هزم الجيش المصري في حماة. احتل نبوكذنصر الثاني مدينة عسقلان، وكذلك جزءاً من يهوذا، عام ٦٠٥ ق. م. وفي أواخر ٦٠١ ق. م، غزا مصر ثم عاد إلى بابل. بعد انتصاره في شمال الجزيرة العربية. في شتاء ٥٩٨ ق. م. قاد جيشه بنفسه ضد اورشليم وفي عام ٥٩٧ ق. م سقطت المدينة في يده، وتمّ ترحيل ملكها يوياقيم مع بلاطه والعديد من السكان البارزين إلى بابل. ثم عيّن نبوكذنصر الثاني اليهودي ماتنيا مسئولا عن القدس عام ٥٩٠ ق م . قاد ماتنيا ثورة ضد نبوكذنصر الثاني لكنه قُتل. تمّ تدمير القدس نفسها، بعد حصار مرير(٥٨٩-٥٧٨ ق. م ).

تمّ تسجيل دمار أورشليم في الكتاب المقدس (ملوك الثاني ٢٤:٦-١٥، أخبار الأيام الثاني ٣٦: ٩-١٠ وإرميا ٢٢: ٢٤- ٣٠؛ ٢٧:٢٠). تمّ نهب هيكل أورشليم، وأخذ عشرة آلاف أسير، وتم ترحيل النبلاء والحرفيين والعائلة المالكة إلى بابل.

وفقاً لإرميا (٢٥: ٢٧-٢٩)، لا شيء كان قادراً على إيقاف نجاح نبوكذنصر الثاني لأنه جاء من الله نفسه (انظر أيضاً: إرميا ٣٢: ١-٥؛ ٣٧: ١-١١؛ ٣٨: ١٤-٢٣). كما يذكر إرميا عمليات الترحيل الثلاثة لسبط يهوذا على يد نبوكذنصر الثاني. حدث الأول في ٥٩٨ ق. م. عندما تمّ ترحيل ٣٠٢٣ شخصاً، والثاني حدث في ٥٨٧ ق. م، عندما تمّ ترحيل ٨٣٢ شخصاً. وحدث الثالث في عام ٥٨٢ ق. م. عندما تم ترحيل ٧٥٥ شخصاً. وبلغ عدد المرحلين ٤٦١٠. نظرًا لأن طريق القوافل من القدس إلى بابل كان يبلغ طوله ٩٥٠ ميلاً، فإن هذا الاختطاف الكبير لمواطني القدس لا بد أنه كان عملاً منظماً للغاية. قال النبي حزقيال (٢١:٢٤) بأن الله نفسه وجّه نبوكذنصر الثاني ليضرب اورشليم.

من المثير للاهتمام، وفقاً لسفر دانيال، أن نبوخذ نصر الثاني كان خصم الله (دانيال الفصول ١-٤). ولكن، نظرًا لعدم وجود دعم مستقل لسنوات الجنون السبع لنبوخذ نصر الثاني، يمكننا أن نستنتج أن القصة ربما تكون تفسيراً لاحقاً وخيالياً لنصوص معينة تتعلق بنبونيدوس الغريب الأطوار، آخر ملوك الكلدانيين الذي هجر بابل لعقد من الزمان للعيش في تيماء في شبه الجزيرة العربية (٥٤٥ ق. م).

فرض نبوكذنصر الثاني حصاراً فاشلاً على مدينة صور لمدة ثلاثة عشر عاماً (٥٨٥-٥٧٣ ق. م)، لكن حملته ضد مصر (٥٧٢-٥٦٩ ق. م) كانت أكثر نجاحاً. هُزم

ثرية ومستقرة سياسياً، والتي كانت على مدى الثمانين عامًا التالية القوة الرئيسية في غرب آسيا.

## الملوك الكلدان الخمسة
### ١- نبوبولاسر (٦٢٥-٦٠٥ ق.م)

في عهد آشور بانيبال، ملك آشور (٦٦٨-٦٢٦ ق. م) أسس كلداني يُدعى نابوبولاسار الأسرة البابلية الحادية والثلاثين من بلدة أوروك. قاد ثورة ضد الآشوريين وطردهم أولاً من أوروك، ثم خارج بابل نفسها بحلول عام ٦٢٦ ق. م. كان أول ملك كلداني يستعيد استقلاله المطلق عن بابل. أصبح نبوبولاسار، وهو من نسل مرودخ بلادان، حاكماً ذا قوة ونفوذ عظيمين. انضمّ إلى قوات الملك الميدي سياكساريس، وفي عام ٦١٢ ق. م، استولى على نينوى ثم حاران. سقطت آخر بؤرة استيطانية آشورية (٦٠٩ ق. م) في ذلك الوقت هرب آشور أوباليت الثاني (٦١١-٦٠٩ق. م) آخر الملوك الآشوريين إلى الجنوب في انتظار حلفائه المصريين. انضمت القوات المصرية بقيادة الفرعون نخو الثاني إلى فلول الجيش الآشوري في كركميش وهاجموا الأمير الكلداني المتوج نبوخذ نصر الأول في ربيع ٦٠٥ ق. م بينما كانت الخسائر كبيرة في كلا الجانبين (إرميا ٤٦:١٢)، هُزمت القوات المصرية والآشورية بشكل حاسم. وتقهقرت قواتهم وانسحبوا وهم في حالة فوضى، وطاردهم الجيش الكلداني عبر سوريا. توفي نبوبولاسر الأول في بابل في ٧ سبتمبر ٦٠٥ ق.م. وصلت نبوكذنصر الثاني أخبار وفاة والده في بيلوسيوم. وخلال أسبوعين، عاد من الحدود المصرية إلى بابل حيث تولى الحكم.

### ٢- نبوكذنصر الثاني الامبراطور العظيم (٦٠٥-٥٦٢ ق.م)

(باللغة الأكادية: نابو - أيل - أوسور: «الله نابو حافظ الابن»

سمّى نابوبولاسار ابنه الأكبر على اسم الملك الشهير لأسرة إيسين الثانية الذي توفي عام ١١٢٦ ق. م، وأصبح ابنه نبوكذنصر الثاني أشهر ملوك الإمبراطورية البابلية الجديدة. واصلَ إقامة مشاريع البناء الكثيرة مثل والده. بحلول عام ٦٠٥ ق. م، كان قد سيطر على كل سوريا وفلسطين (إرميا ٤٦: ٢-٦).

أنشأ الكلدانيون عدداً من الدول التي قاومت الانقراض والاندماج خلال الفتح الآشوري في القرنين الثامن والسابع قبل الميلاد.

لا يُعرف سوى القليل عن أول ملك كلداني لبابل، الذي خلفه مَلكا آخر من البحر، إريبا مردوخ (٧٧٠ ق. م). يبدو أنه قد حقق بعض النجاح في تخليص الجوار المباشر لبابل وبورسيبا من الآراميين الذين كانوا يزحفون باستمرار. يذكر الملوك الكلدانيون اللاحقون إيريبا مردوخ باعتباره المؤسس الحقيقي لسلالتهم. وخلفه نبوكدنصر عام ٧٤٧ ق. م.

ان هذا الوقت كان إيذانا ببدء عهد جديد في تاريخ بابل. ومن ثم، تمّ الاحتفاظ بسجلات دقيقة للأحداث التاريخية بشكل منهجي. كانت «أخبار الأيام» هذه سرداً لخلافة ملوك بابل. كما أنها تحتوي على العديد من الروايات عن الملاحظات الفلكية. هذا هو السبب في اعتبار «عصر نبوناصر» نقطة تحول في تاريخ العلوم. في الواقع، أصبح مصطلح «كلداني» مرادفًا لمصطلح «عالم الفلك». بعد وفاة نبوناصر، حدث تمرد في بابل، مما أدى إلى مقتل ابنه وتولي الجيش الآشوري زمام الأمور.

بعد وفاة الملك الآشوري شلمناصير، وصل ملك كلداني، حاكم عائلة بيت ياكين، إلى السلطة في بابل (اقرأ إشعياء ٣٩: ١-٢ / ٢ ملوك ٢٠: ١٢-١٣). استولى مرودخ بلدان على العرش البابلي عام ٧٢١ قبل الميلاد، وظل يحتفظ به حتى عام ٧١٠ ق. م. (اقرأ ٢ ملوك ٢٠: ١٢-١٣ / ٢ أخ ٣٢:٣١). أجبر الحاكم مرودخ بلدان على الفرار إلى الأهوار، حيث أعيد ملكًا لعشيرة بيت ياكين، تاركًا بابل تحت سيطرة المسؤولين الآشوريين.

حوالي عام ٧٠٠ (ق. م). حاول بن عبري، وهو كلداني آخر، الوصول إلى السلطة في بابل. وبعد سبع سنوات، حاول مشيزيب مردوخ استعادة الاستقلال عن الآشوريين، لكنه فرّ بحراً وتوفي هناك.

بحلول نهاية النصف الأول من القرن السابع قبل الميلاد، ظهر حاكم غامض اسمه كالدالانو ملكاً على بابل (٦٤٩-٦٢٧ ق. م). طوال هذه الفترة ظلّ الكلدان أقوياء، مما خلق تهديداً للسلطة الآشورية، التي كانت على وشك الانهيار.

استولى مَلكا كلداني يدعى نبوبولاسار على عرش بابل. أسس إمبراطورية كلدانية

# الفصـل الثانـي
## الإمبراطوريــة الكلدانيــة – البابليــون الجـدد
## آخر دولة مَلكية في بلاد ما بين النهرين (٦٢٦-٥٣٩ ق. م)

تمّ ذكر بلاد تسمى الكلدان، مع سكانها الكلدان حوالي القرن التاسع قبل الميلاد. جاءت هذه الإشارة في عهد الملك الأشوري شلمناصر الثالث (٨٥٠ ق. م). جاء شلمناصر لمساعدة حلفائه ضد الآراميين، وفي طريقه التقى بشعوب أخرى، من بينها الكلدان. هذا هو أول ذكر للأشخاص الذين لعبوا دوراً رائداً في التاريخ.

جاء ذكر الكلدان، كدولة، في حوليات الملك الآشوري آشور ناصربال الثاني(٨٨٤-٨٥٩ ق. م) قبل هذا الوقت، كانت المنطقة الجغرافية تسمى «أراضي البحر». أغار الملك شلمناصر الثالث (٨٥٨-٨٤٢ ق. م) من آشور على المنطقة حوالي (٨٥٠ ق. م) وصل إلى الخليج العربي. وأطلق على البلاد اسم «**بحر الكلدان**».

بحلول نهاية القرن الثاني عشر قبل الميلاد، كانت الأسرة الرابعة والعشرون من الكيشيين قد انتهى حكمهم في بلاد ما بين النهرين. أعقب ذلك فترة من الارتباك، بينما كان الآشوريون يسيطرون عادة على بلاد بابل. والآراميون، (الشعب السامي) حاولوا أيضاً محاصرة السلطة. أخيراً، سيطر القادة البابليون على الآشوريين وأعلنوا سلطتهم في بابل.

عاش هؤلاء الكلدان بين الأهوار والبحيرات على طول المجرى السفلي لنهري دجلة والفرات. كان تنظيمهم قبلياً، وكان كل «بَيتا» كلداني (منزل، عائلة، عشيرة) تحت قيادة مَلكا (ملك). كانت القوة السياسية لكل فرد من مالكا مسألة تتعلق بشكل كبير بالقدرة الشخصية والهيبة. أكبر القبائل، بيث داكوري، كانت تقع جنوب بورسيبا، ليست بعيدة عن بابل.

إلى الجنوب كانت هناك بيث أموكاي، وعلى طول نهر دجلة إلى الشرق على الحدود مع بيث أيلان يكين عاشت القبائل الكلدانية في منطقة مزدهرة بأشجار النخيل واحتفظوا بقطعان كبيرة من الخيول والماشية. كانوا تجارًا يتحكمون في طرق التجارة الجنوبية حيث حملوا الخشب الأبنوس والعاج وجلود الأفيال والذهب.

تكوين ١١: ٢٧-٣١ «هذا هو سجل تارح. أصبح تارح والد إبراهيم وناحور وحاران. مات حاران قبل والده تارح في موطنه أور الكلدانيين. أخذ تارح ابنه إبراهيم وكنته ساراي وأخرجهما من أور الكلدانيين ليذهبوا إلى أرض كنعان. ثم في تكوين ١٢: ١ نقرأ، «دعا الرب الله إبراهيم قائلاً: اخرج من أقارب أبيك ومن بيت أبيك إلى الأرض التي سأريكها». في تكوين ١٥: ٧ قال الرب لإبراهيم: «أنا الرب الذي أتى بك من أور الكلدانيين لأعطيك هذه الأرض». يعطي إنجيل القديس متى ١: ١ السجل العائلي ليسوع المسيح بأنه نسل إبراهيم من مواطن أور الكلدانيين.

ظهرت الكتابة، وتحديداً الرموز المجردة للكتابة المسمارية والتي تُعرف أيضاً باسم الكتابة الإسفينية (الخط المسماري)، في بلاد ما بين النهرين حوالي 3500 ق.م. إن هذا فتح الباب أمام التاريخ المكتوب والصيغ الكتابية الأخرى، بما في ذلك خريطة العالم.

بدأ علم التنجيم في الألفية الثالثة قبل الميلاد، في أور الكلدان، على الرغم من وجود أدلة مبكرة، وجدت على ألواح طينية تظهر أن علم التنجيم بدأ قبل ذلك في بابل. تمّ بناء الزقورات في بلاد ما بين النهرين المصنوعة من ألواح الآجر الطيني، المشابهة لتلك المستخدمة في برج بابل، لمراقبة النجوم وموقع الأبراج.

لا يزال علم الكونيات القديم في بلاد ما بين النهرين أساس علم الفلك الحالي. شمش، إله الشمس والمشترِع، كان يحكم النهار، بينما إله القمر، سين، يحكم الليل. تحركا على طول خط الاستواء السماوي الذي سُمي على اسم إله آخر، آنو. ومن ثم، فإن تأثير الشمس والقمر على طول مسير الشمس يعود إلى بابل. لكن في البداية، تنبأ علم التنجيم فقط بمصير الملك والدولة، وليس عن مصير الأفراد. خلال الفترة الهلنستية (من القرن الرابع إلى القرن الأول قبل الميلاد)، جمع الإغريق بين علم التنجيم البابلي والمصري وبين الرياضيات وعلم الفلك الخاصين بهم، وبذلك شكلوا النظام المستخدم حاليا في الغرب.

في أور الكلدان، يحتمل أن السومريين قد صنعوا الجعة (البيرة). يقول العلماء إنهم وجدوا أول دليل كيميائي معروف على أن القدماء شربوا الجعة: رواسب صفراء شاحبة في داخل جرة عمرها أكثر من 5000 عام. أشارت الاختبارات إلى أن الرواسب كانت عبارة عن كالسيوم، أكسالات، وهي مادة تستقر عند تخزين البيرة أو تخميرها في حوالي 3100 ق.م، وجد علماء الآثار العديد من هذه المواقع في بلاد ما بين النهرين. وذكر الباحثون أن «الرواسب الصفراء الموجودة في الأخاديد ربما تكون قد وُضعت هناك لإزالة أكسالات الكالسيوم المر من البيرة».

وفقاً لكتاب سفر التكوين، فإن أور الكلدانيين، الواقعة في دلتا نهري دجلة والفرات، جنوب بلاد ما بين النهرين هي مسقط رأس إبراهيم التقليدي. إبراهيم هو أب الديانات الثلاث اليهودية والمسيحية والإسلام، والتي تضم ثلث سكان العالم اليوم. نقرأ ما يلي في

اريدو ٥٠٠٠ ق. م

في الجنوب: عوبيد ٤٥٠٠ ق. م - أوروك ٣٥٠٠ ق. م

**الأحداث المسجلة من الألفية الرابعة إلى الثالثة قبل الميلاد**

تمثل نهاية فترة ما قبل التاريخ نهاية خاصة. حيث بدأ العصر التاريخي بأول ظهور للكتابة. يرجع الفضل إلى السومريين في إنشاء هذا النظام الأول للكتابة حوالي ٣٢٠٠ ق. م.

اعطت بلاد ما بين النهرين عددا من الأمور المهمة، من بينها المكان الذي تم فيه إنشاء الشكل الأول للكتابة واستخدامه، وحيث تم اختراع العجلات لأول مرة، وتمّ تشريع أولى القوانين الشهيرة، من قبل ملك بابل المشهور، حمورابي. وأشهر القوانين التي سنّها تجدها في مسلة حمورابي. أعطت بلاد ما بين النهرين القديمة للعالم مبادئ الرياضيات الأساسية والساعة ٦٠ دقيقة والدائرة ٣٦٠ درجة وعلم الفلك وعلم التنجيم وأخيرًا هي المكان الذي ازدهرت فيه الآرامية، لغة المسيح والعهد الجديد، وأصبحت لغة مشتركة للشرق الأوسط في القرن السابع قبل الميلاد.

يؤكد علم الآثار أنه حوالي ٣٥٠٠ ق. م، نشأت أول مجموعة مدن في العالم في بلاد ما بين النهرين القديمة. كانت مدناً تحمل أسماء مثل أور (الكلدانيين) وإريدو وأوروك (والتي قد يكون الاسم الحالي للعراق قد اشتق منها). انضمت دول المدن إلى ممالك تحت حكم أقوى الحكام، الذين قاموا بإنشاء امبراطورية كبيرة، كانت الإمبراطورية الأولى - إمبراطورية سرجون الأكدى العظيمة، وقد توغلت جيوشه في لبنان والأناضول (تركيا) وبلاد فارس حوالي ٢٣٠٠ ق. م.

لقد لعبت التكنولوجيا أيضا دورها في بلاد ما بين النهرين، وقد مكّن الملك سرجون المدى الطويل للقوس المركّب من الدخول في عصر الصواريخ الأول. بدأ علم المعادن، عندما تم اختراع أول محراث. لم يساعد المحراث في ملء الحقول بالحبوب فحسب، بل ساعد أيضاً في صنع الأسلحة. تمّ إنشاء عدد من الصناعات المختلفة بعد تأسيس علم المعادن، على سبيل المثال تمّ استخدام عجلة الخزاف في صنع العربة، واستخدم الحديد والبرونز في صنع السيوف والرماح للقتال.

# الفصــل الأول
# بلــد الكلــدان

إن المجتمع الكلداني في سانديكو، كاليفورنيا، هو مجتمع مسيحي كاثوليكي هاجر من بلاد ما بين النهرين - الأرض الواقعة بين نهري دجلة والفرات أو «العراق» الحديث. وهو جزء من الهلال الخصيب، والذي كان «مهد الحضارات» حيث ولدت الأنظمة السياسية والقضائية والدينية والعسكرية التي وجهت المجتمعات القديمة على مسار من شأنه أن يؤدي في النهاية إلى نظام العالم الحديث المعقد مثل الأمم والدول والبلدان.

إن كتاب التكوين يضع جنّة عدن في بلاد ما بين النهرين، وثمّ أيضاً تمّ اختيار حدائق بابل المعلقة العظيمة التي أقامها الإمبراطور الكلداني نبوكذنصر الثاني نحو ٦٠٠ ق. م لامرأته أميتاس، كواحدة من عجائب الدنيا السبع.

### أحـداث مـا قبـل التاريـخ

إن معرفتنا الحالية ببلاد ما بين النهرين القديمة، مهد الحضارة، تعتمد بشكل حصري تقريباً على دراسة الوثائق المكتوبة والتحف التي عثر عليها علماء الآثار من أكوام المدن المدمرة في بلاد ما بين النهرين خلال المائة وخمسين سنة الماضية.

عبر العصور القديمة، لعبت حضارة سكان بلاد ما بين النهرين دوراً رائداً في السياسة والفنون والعلوم والفلسفة والدين والآداب في الشرق الأدنى والعالم.

لا يُعرف الكثير عن المستوطنين الأوائل في بلاد ما بين النهرين. توجد آثار للصيادين ومربي الماشية منذ عشرة آلاف سنة قبل الميلاد. وكذلك مزارعو الحبوب والنباتات الأخرى، وتم اكتشاف بقايا قرى مأهولة تعود إلى ٦٠٠٠ ق. م. وبحسب المؤرخين، فإن أقدم قريتين في بلاد ما بين النهرين هما حسونة بالقرب من نينوى في شمال بلاد ما بين النهرين وتل سوار بالقرب من سامراء في وسط بلاد ما بين النهرين.

### فيما يلي مراحل ثقافة ما قبل التاريخ الرئيسية:

في الشمال: جرمو ٧٠٠٠ ق. م - حسونة ٦٠٠٠ ق. م - سامراء ٥,٥٠٠ ق. م -

**حزقيال ٣٠:٢٤** «قال الرب: سأقوي ذراع ملك بابل واجعل سيفي بيده واكسر ذراعي فرعون» والنبي. يسمّي الكلدانيين جبابرة.

**حزقيال ٣٢:١١** «قال الرب: ان سيف ملك بابل يأتي عليكَ فأسقط جمهورك بسيوف جبابرة».

**دانيال النبي** عاش في بلاط نبوكذنصر في بابل كمستشار. في كتابه من فصل ١-٤ معظم الحديث هو عن نبوكذنصر. اجمل ما كتب: ان نبوكذنصر بعد مشاهدته كيف أن الله خلَّص من النار الشباب الثلاثة، صلّى قائلاً: «أنا نبوكذنصر أُسبّح وامجّد ملك السماء الذي جميع أعماله حق وطرقه عادلة».

ما هو عجيب في ما رأينا بان الكتاب المقدس يجعل نبوكذنصر الشخص المفضل لديه حيث إن الله ساعده وهو من غير الشعب المختار، ليسبي الشعب المختار واستخدمه تعالى لتحقيق مقاصده.

**وعن وصف الجنود الكلدانيين، كتب النبي حبقوق (الذي هو من الأنبياء الصغار توفي عام ٥٨٩ ق . م) قائلاً: (١: ٦- ١٠)** «هكذا قال الرب أنا أقيم الكلدانيين الشعب الذي يسير في عرض الأرض أسرع من النمور هي خيولهم وأسرع من الذئاب في المساء. خيلهم تقفز وفرسانهم يأتون من بعيد. يطيرون كالنسر مسرعا بالابتلاع. يأتي كل منهم من الشرق، وبداية ظهورهم المشترك هي رياح عاصفة تتراكم على الأسرى مثل الرمل. يسخرون من الملوك والأمراء هم أضحوكة. يضحكون على أي حصن. يمرّون كالريح ويعبروا».

# المقدمــــة

في الكتاب المقدس بعهديه القديم والجديد، اسم الكلدان مهم جداً. حيث ذكر اسم الكلدان ٧٠ مرة، واسم الامبراطور الكلداني نبوكذنصر ١١١ مرة، واسم كلدو ١٤ مرة. وكلداني ١٣ مرة وأور الكلدانيين ٤ مرات. وبابل ٣٠٠ مرة والبابليون ٢١ مرة.

اليكم بعض المقتطفات من اقوال الأنبياء. منهم الانبياء الكبار:

١- اشعيا توفي عام ٧١٠ ق.م.

٢- إرميا توفي عام ٥٨٦ ق.م.

٣- حزقيال ٥٧١ ق.م. توفي في بابل.

٤- دانيال توفي في بابل عام ٥٣٥ ق.م.

هؤلاء الأنبياء ذكروا في نبوآتهم الكلدانيين وامبراطورهم نبوكذنصر. الاثنان الأولان كتبا وتنبأا في اورشليم اما الاثنان الاخيران فقد رافقا المسبيين في شبابهما إلى بابل وعاشا وتنبأا وماتا في بابل عاصمة الكلدانيين.

**إشعيا ١٩:١٣** يسمّي بابل زينة الممالك وبهاء وفخر الكلدانيين.

**إرميا ٨:٢٥** «يقول الرب هوذا انا ارسل نبوكذنصر ملك بابل عبدي وآتي به إلى هذه الأرض التي سأجعلها أرضا خربة وتستعبد لملك بابل سبعون سنة».

**إرميا ٨:٣٧** هكذا قال الرب: «إن الكلدانيين الذين حاربوا مصر وانتصروا سيأتون الى اورشليم ويحرقوها».

**إرميا ٦:٣٨** ألقى رؤساء اليهود ارميا في الجب في اورشليم ولما وصل نبوكذنصر رفعه من البئر وحرره.

**إرميا ٧:٥١** أفضل تلخيص للحكم الكلداني جاء في وصفه لبابل الكلدانيين على أنها «كأس ذهبي في يد الرب تسكر كل الأرض».

**حزقيال ١١:١٧** كتب «كانت إلي كلمة الرب قائلاً: قل لبيت التمرّد: ها إن ملك بابل قد أتى الى اورشيم ويأخذ ملكها وعظماء الأرض».

**حزقيال ٣:٢١** «قال الرب: سيف ملك بابل سيكون على يهوذا وأوشليم».

أنظر ٢مل فصل ٢٥

**حزقيال ١٩:٢٩** «هكذا قال الرب: هاءنذا اعطي نبوكذنصر ملك بابل ارض مصر».

# كلمــة اولــى

الأب ميخائيل بزّي ابنٌ أصيل للأمة الكلدانية، وكاهن مخلص لكنيسته ولهويتها المشرقية. إن هذا الكتاب تسجيل جامع لوضع الكلدان في العالم في هذه الحقبة التاريخية، كتبه إبنٌ وفيّ خَـدَمَ شعبه بأمانة لفترة تزيد على سبعة وخمسين عاماً. محطاتها الأساسية: تلكيف، ديترويت، وسانديكو.

المطران سرهد يوسپ جَمّو
٦ - ت١-٢٠٢١

# المحتوى

كلمــة اولــى ................... ٣

المقدمـــة ................... ٥

الفصل الأول: بلد الكلدان ................... ٩

الفصـل الثانـي: الإمبراطورية الكلدانية – البابليون الجدد – آخر مَلكية في بلاد ما بين النهرين ................... ١٣

الفصل الثالـث: الكنيسة الكلدانية ................... ٢١

الفصل الرابـع: الكنيسة الكلدانية في العالم ................... ٢٣

الفصل الخامس: الكنيسة الكلدانية في الولايات المتحدة ................... ٢٥

الفصل السادس: الكلدان الكاثوليك في سان دييكو ................... ٢٨

الفصل السابع: الكنائس الشرقية الكاثوليكية ................... ٣٧

الفصل الثامـن: الطقس الكلداني ................... ٤٠

الفصل التاسـع: الآرامية - لغة – الكلدان ................... ٤٢

الملحـق: رسالة سام كمو ................... ٤٤

# الامّة الكلدانية

# ماضيها وحاضرها

تأليف
القسّ ميخائيل جّجو بزّي
سان دييكو / كاليفورنيا
٢٠٢٢